Time for HOMEWORK

Colleen Timoshenko

4

Book 4

Hunter Education Nightingale

HUNTER
EDUCATION
NIGHTINGALE

Time for Homework - Book 4

Published by:
Hunter Education Nightingale
ABN: 69 055 798 626
PO Box 547
Warners Bay NSW 2282
Ph: 0417 658 777
email: sales@huntereducationnightingale.com.au
paul@huntereducationnightingale.com.au
www.huntereducationnightingale.com.au

Cover Design: Doriana Berkovic

National Library of Australia Card No.
and ISBN 978 - 1 - 922242 - 28 - 0

RECYCLING

When the program is completed and the paper no longer wanted, be sure to have it recycled. The time and care taken to recycle may help save a tree and maintain our environment.

F E D C B A
19 18 17 16 15 14

Time for Homework

Book 4

About this Book

Time for Homework Book 4 is the fifth in a series of seven books written to help reinforce many of the concepts, skills and understanding needed for today's school curriculum.

The series is designed as a user-friendly resource to improve a student's reading skills, knowledge of grammar, accuracy in spelling and improved word knowledge through word building activities. Questions covering the New Mathematics Curriculum complete each unit.

The book contains 30 units of work and one unit can be attempted each week. Each unit addresses the subjects outlined above and covers topics in today's environment which are relevant to the new Australian Curriculum for English and Mathematics.

As the child gains a better knowledge of language; reading, interpreting and responding to the written text develops and improves. Knowledge of grammar, punctuation and spelling, as well as mathematics is acquired by completing the set activities.

While *Time for Homework* treats many of the topics presented in the school curriculum, it is a summary only of those subjects. This book is fun to use at home, with the child, as a resource, to develop and improve learning.

Message to Parents

With *Time for Homework, Book 4*, your child should not need help with reading or the explanation of instructions. As a parent you are asked to support your child's learning but resist the temptation to provide answers. By all means, read a word for your child if necessary and then support him/her to gain a better knowledge about the word and its meaning. This reassures the child and enables one to become a more independent learner. As the child works through the book your encouragement may be all that is needed.

Regular homework helps your child develop skills which will assist in the learning process and improve confidence over time. A confident and skilled learner will enjoy school.

Praise your child at all times because you are the ideal support person in your child's life. Use this book together to make the learning process more meaningful for both of you.

Time for Homework, Book 4 is designed as a fun book for home use. Enjoy the journey!

A Cyclonic Disturbance

It was the frightening noise that woke us. And before we could recognise what it was, it happened again. And again! Now the wind was howling and the night was exploding with each passing minute. It felt as though the whole house was threatening to blow apart with each gust of wind. What was causing this rising fear in us? We certainly had never experienced anything like it before.

As usual, mum was trying to calm everyone. The power had gone off and dad was trying to find a torch.

"Oh no!" dad cried, "there's no battery in this torch!"

It was then that we knew a dark night would be our fate and we would just have to wait until the storm passed. A mini-cyclone had hit the coast and caused power lines to fall, trees to uproot and ships to drag their anchor. The force of the wind had driven one of the ships ashore and it was now beached on our favourite swimming spot.

It took many days to repair the damage but worst of all it took even longer to move the enormous cargo ship beached on the shore.

Understanding

Use the narrative to answer each question.

a. What was the 'frightening noise' everyone heard? ____________

b. Why was the house in darkness? ____________

c. What was mum trying to do? ____________

d. What was dad's dilemma? ____________

e. What other words are used for 'mini-cyclone'? ____________

Interpreting

Circle **T** (true) or **F** (false) to answer correctly.

a. The events happened before everyone went to bed.	**T**	**F**
b. The night was howling and the wind was exploding.	**T**	**F**
c. A ship had dragged its anchor and beached itself.	**T**	**F**
d. It is a good idea to keep an emergency kit on hand.	**T**	**F**
e. The wind is given a human characteristic.	**T**	**F**

Language

Find the **adjective** that describes each noun in the narrative and write it on the line.

a. ____________ noise b. ____________ wind

c. ____________ night d. ____________ minute

e. ____________ fear f. ____________ night

g. ____________ ____________ spot

Spelling

Look, cover, write, check each word.

noise ______ ☐

scary ______ ☐

minute ______ ☐

usual ______ ☐

battery ______ ☐

knew ______ ☐

fate ______ ☐

cyclone ______ ☐

anchor ______ ☐

cargo ______ ☐

Word Building

Words ending in '**y**' change '**y**' to '**i**' to add '**er**'.

scary ______

happy ______

funny ______

merry ______

steady ______

pretty ______

Edit the following text.

hes book is overdew buy now

______

______

Sentences

Use a **time connective**, from the word bank, to complete each sentence.

WORD BANK: before noon after dinner in the morning during the night

a. As usual, ______ we watched TV then went to bed.

b. The cyclonic depression hit us ______ .

c. ______ everyone went out to look at the damage.

d. The electricity was restored to our house ______ .

Place Value

1. Write the number on each abacus.

a. 4382

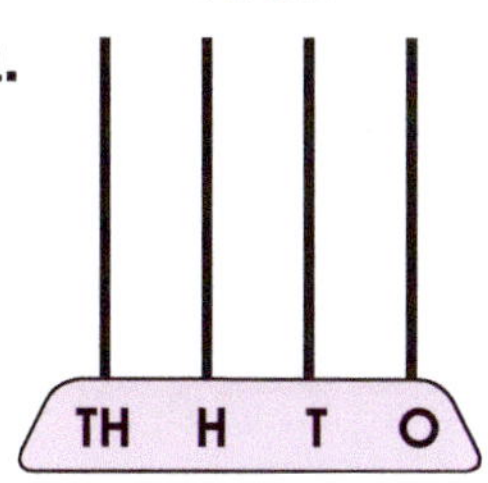

☐

b. 3567

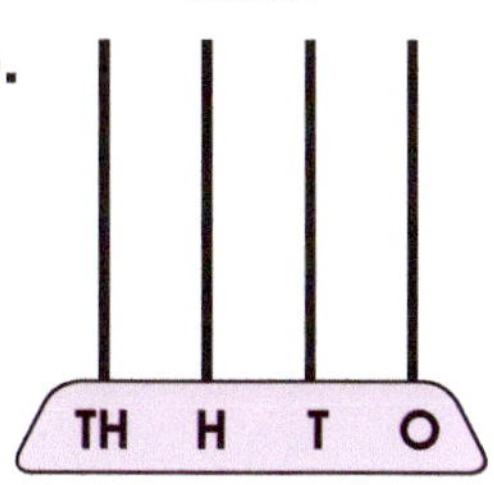

☐

2. Write each number using numerals.

a. Four thousand, seven hundred and sixty-seven ☐

b. Eight thousand, two hundred and forty-five ☐

c. Nine thousand, six hundred and seventy-one ☐

Addition

1. Complete each addition sentence.

a. $6 + 25 + 4 =$ ☐

b. $48 + 32 =$ ☐

c. $9 + 27 + 11 =$ ☐

d. $39 + 12 + 21 =$ ☐

e. $62 + 28 + 3 =$ ☐

f. $44 + 32 + 24 =$ ☐

2. Add the numbers.

a. $625 + 145 =$ ______

b. $384 + 205 =$ ______

c. $346 + 233 =$ ______

d. $1363 + 3234 =$ ______

e. $6145 + 1723 =$ ______

The Echidna

The echidna is a warm-blooded mammal with the mother producing milk to feed her young.

Echidnas are also called spiny ant-eaters. They have a coat of long, sharp spines which dig into people. So, if holding an echidna it is always a good idea to have a pair of gloves to protect you from getting hurt.

This animal has a long beak and a sticky tongue which it uses to get into termite nests and gather the ants to eat.

A female echidna has a pouch where she keeps her eggs and then her young. When the eggs hatch she feeds her young on her milk.

Echidnas are monotremes meaning they lay eggs and suckle their young. The only other monotreme is the platypus. Both of these animals are native to Australia.

Understanding

Tick the box if the information is in the text

- **a.** The echidna is found only in Australia. ☐
- **b.** Echidnas are the only animals found in Australia. ☐
- **c.** Spiny ant-eaters have a long beak and sharp spines. ☐
- **d.** You need to wear protective clothing to hold an echidna. ☐
- **e.** There are two monotremes in Australia. ☐

Interpreting

Match a word to its meaning

WORD BANK: indigenous, termite, suckle, mammal, female, hatch, gooey, platypus

a. ant ____________________ **b.** sticky ____________________

c. to drink ____________________ **d.** native ____________________

e. mother ____________________ **f.** breed ____________________

g. flat foot ____________________ **h.** milk producing ____________________

Language

Select a better **adjective** than the one in brackets from the word bank, to **describe the noun**.

WORD BANK: huge, large, scrumptious, answered, replied, tiring

a. Dad had a (big) ____________ hat. **b.** The (big) ____________ shoes were wet.

c. It was a (nice) ____________ day. **d.** We had a (nice) ____________ lunch.

e. We (said) ____________ no to him. **f.** "It was easy," (said) ____________ Tony.

Spelling

Unit 2

Look, cover, write, check each word.

mammal	______________	☐
produces	______________	☐
people	______________	☐
gloves	______________	☐
protect	______________	☐
animal	______________	☐
tongue	______________	☐
young	______________	☐
suckle	______________	☐
native	______________	☐

Word Building

Match a list word to its meaning

a. worn on the hand ______________

b. youthful, small ______________

c. save from harm ______________

d. an organ in the body ______________

e. to nurse or to drink ______________

f. an original inhabitant ______________

g. feeds from its mother ______________

h. tribe, race or nation ______________

Unjumble this word - **meontomer**

____

Sentences

Match the beginnings and endings to make **simple statements**.

a. The echidna	**e.** lays eggs
b. Echidnas	**f.** has a pouch
c. A female echidna	**g.** is a warm-blooded mammal
d. A monotreme	**h.** have long beaks and sticky tongues

Odds and Evens

1. Colour the **odd** numbers.

6	9	7	8	15	31
24	18	13	12	19	99

2. Write the **odd** numbers **between** 20 and 30.

____ ____ ____ ____ ____

3. Write the **even** numbers **between** 40 and 50.

40 ____ ____ ____ ____ 50

Subtraction

1. Complete each subtraction sentence.

a. 28 - 7 = ☐ **b.** 64 - 18 = ☐

c. 83 - 25 = ☐ **d.** 39 - 27 = ☐

e. 48 - 36 = ☐ **f.** 94 - 36 = ☐

2. Complete these subtractions.

a. 465 - 213 = ____ **b.** 852 - 130 = ____ **c.** 489 - 167 = ____

Early Space Exploration

For many years man wondered if there was anything beyond Earth. The atmosphere fades about 200km beyond the Earth's surface and there is just space. There is no air or gravity in space and humans would find it impossible to live there without the aid of a special space suit.

In 1957, the Russians sent a man-made object, called Sputnik 1, into space. Later in November 1957, Sputnik 2 was launched. This satellite was the first to orbit the Earth and it carried a dog called Laika (like-ă). The reason for this journey was to find out if humans could survive in space.

So in 1959 both America and Russia tried to get a spacecraft to the Moon. However, Luna 2 crashed into the moon and it took another ten years before a safe moon landing was achieved. Then on 12 April 1961, the Russian Cosmonaut, Yuri Gagarin, became the first man in space in Vostok 1. In 1963 the first woman in space was another Russian Cosmonaut called Valentina Tereshkova (Tĕ – resh-ko-va).

During the '60s both America and Russia continued their space explorations and successfully landed un-manned space crafts on the Moon. But on 20 July 1969, the American astronauts, Neil Armstrong and then Buzz Aldrin stepped out of Apollo 11 and walked on the Moon.

Understanding
Shade the bubble for the best answer

a. Where does the atmosphere begin?
- ◯ from the Earth's surface
- ◯ on the Earth's surface
- ◯ beyond the Earth's surface
- ◯ around the Moon

b. The first person in space was
- ◯ Neil Armstrong
- ◯ Yuri Gagarin
- ◯ Buzz Aldrin
- ◯ an American

c. Who tried to get to the Moon first?
- ◯ Russia
- ◯ America
- ◯ Yuri Gagarin
- ◯ Both America and Russia

d. What is another name for 'sputnik'
- ◯ Lunar 2
- ◯ Vostok 1
- ◯ satellite
- ◯ rocket

Interpreting
Write an answer to each question

a. Which country reached the Moon first? ______________________________

b. What name is given to a Russian space man? ______________________________

c. Who was the first woman in space? ______________________________

d. From what country did she come? ______________________________

e. What was special about Sputnik 2? ______________________________

Language
Match these two **acronyms** about space travel to their meaning.

ISS **NASA**

a. National Aeronautics and Space Administration ______________________________

b. International Space Station ______________________________

Spelling

Look, cover, write, check each word.

years	____________	☐
wonder	____________	☐
gravity	____________	☐
special	____________	☐
object	____________	☐
launch	____________	☐
survive	____________	☐
achieve	____________	☐
continue	____________	☐
explore	____________	☐

Word Building

Root words - 'aster' from the Greek meaning **star**
Match each word to its meaning

a. asteroid	**g.** study of celestial bodies
d. asterisk	**h.** relating to stars
c. astronomy	**i.** study of the stars on humans
d. astral	**j.** a star-like reference mark
e. astronaut	**k.** small planets orbiting others
f. astrology	**l.** a pilot of a spaceship

Root words - 'kosmo' from the Greek - **the World**
Match each word to its meaning

a. cosmos	**c.** belonging to all parts of the World
b. cosmopolitan	**d.** the physical universe

Sentences

Write the **subject and verb** in each sentence

	SUBJECT	VERB
a. I am going home.	____________	____________
b. Astronauts are American space pilots.	____________	____________
c. "Hello!" cried Jon.	____________	____________
d. Twenty people saw the concert.	____________	____________
e. "Beware," shouted our teacher.	____________	____________

Angles

1. Label each angle as **acute**, **obtuse**, **right**, **reflex** or **straight**.

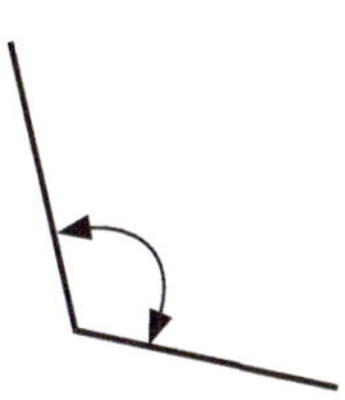

a. ____________

b. ____________

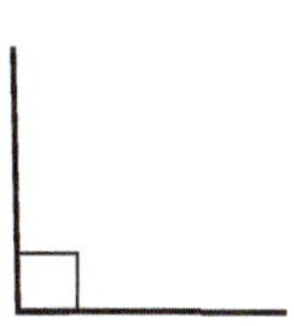

c. ____________

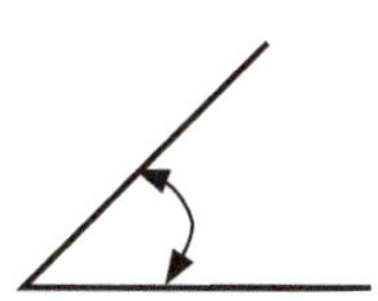

d. ____________

e. ____________

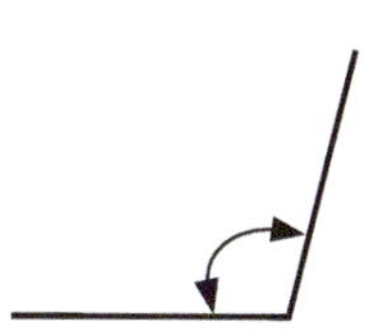

f. ____________

Time

1. Write each time as morning time.

a. Twenty-seven minutes past nine. ____________

b. Twenty-five minutes to eight. ____________

c. six minutes to eleven. ____________

2. Write each time in digital form.

a. 35 minutes past eleven ____________

b. Half past nine ____________

c. 25 past 6 ____________

3. Write the time 30 minutes **before** and **after** these times.

Map Reading

Read this map and answer the questions below.

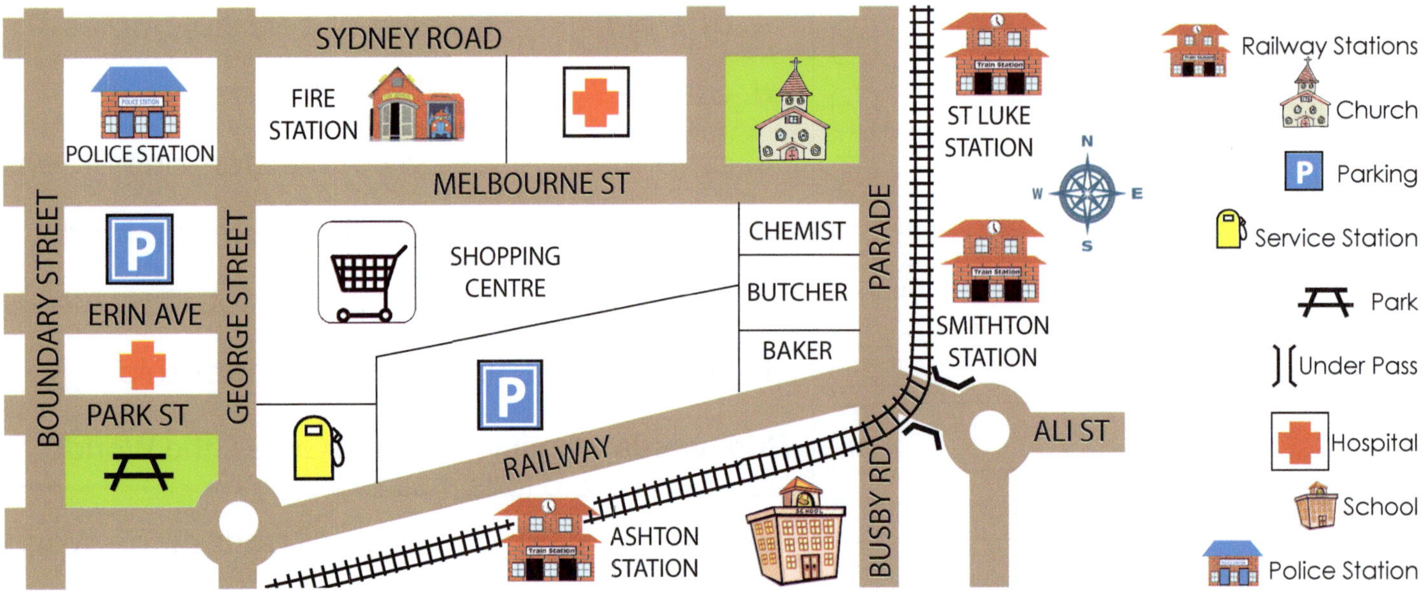

Understanding

Tick the box if you can find this information on the map.

On this map there are:

- a. two hospitals ☐
- b. three sets of traffic lights ☐
- c. a railway line ☐
- d. two railway stations ☐
- e. two schools ☐
- f. one church ☐
- g. a police station ☐
- h. a playing field ☐
- i. a supermarket ☐
- j. two parking places ☐

Interpreting

Write an answer to each question

a. Why is there an underpass on the map? ______

b. Is this a big town? Explain your answer. ______

c. What is the main street in the town? ______

d. Why is it called 'Boundary" Street? ______

e. In what street would you expect to find the most traffic? Explain your answer.

______

Language

Underline the **common nouns** in red and the **proper nouns** in blue in each sentence.

a. Ali and Paris were swimming in the lake until sunset.

b. Will the principal, Mr Green and all the teachers be leaving this year?

c. The fire burnt the house so fast that Sam, the firefighter, was unable to save it.

d. Because the clouds in the sky were black we knew it would rain very soon.

Spelling

Look, cover, write, check each word.

traffic ____________ ☐
lights ____________ ☐
underpass ____________ ☐
boundary ____________ ☐
railway ____________ ☐
supermarket ____________ ☐
hospital ____________ ☐
station ____________ ☐
ambulance ____________ ☐
police ____________ ☐

Word Building

Compound Words - Write as two words

a. Swansea ________ ________
b. railway ________ ________
c. supermarket ________ ________
d. underpass ________ ________
e. highway ________ ________
f. bypass ________ ________
g. Allandale ________ ________
h. Newcastle ________ ________

Write the list word with **four** syllables.

____

Sentences

Circle the letter of the sentences that are **commands**.

a. Sit down!
b. Run quickly!
c. He is a slow reader.
d. Mum went to town.
e. You're fired!
f. Get up now!
g. Will you be next?
h. No, you can't.
i. It is too late for TV.
j. Turn left at the next stop.
k. Go down Railway Parade.
l. You must be quiet.

Partition

1. Write as a whole number each partitioned number.

a. (6x1000)+ (2x100)+ (4x10)+7 = ________
b. (3x1000)+ (1x100)+ (8x10)+6 = ________
c. (4x1000)+ (8x100)+ (9x10)+3 = ________
d. (2x1000)+ (7x100)+ (5x10) = ________

2. Fill in the missing numerals for each number.

a. 62 358 = ☐ x 10 000 + ☐ x 1000 + ☐ x 100 + ☐ x 10 + ☐ x 1

b. 86 594 = ☐ x 10 000 + ☐ x 1000 + ☐ x 100 + ☐ x 10 + ☐ x 1

Multiplying by 4

1. Fill in the 'turn around' sentences about 4.

a. 4 x 3 = ☐ ☐ = 3 x 4
b. 4 x 7 = ☐ ☐ = 7 x 4
c. 4 x 10 = ☐ ☐ = 10 x 4
d. 4 x 8 = ☐ ☐ = 8 x 4

2. Complete the number wheel.

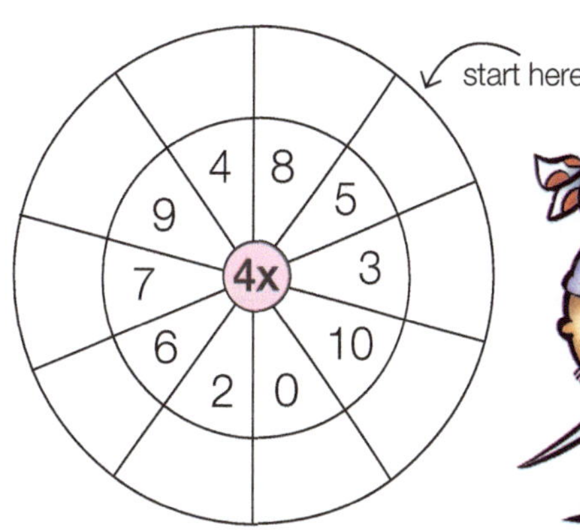

How to Make Rainbow Swirls

Ingredients

2 slices of soft, white bread
Softened Butter
Hundreds and Thousands

Method

1. Butter the bread
2. Cut the crust off each slice
3. Sprinkle hundreds and thousands on the butter
4. Roll the bread firmly in cling wrap
5. Leave bread rolled for 10 minutes
6. Undo bread rolls from the cling wrap
7. Cut bread into 2cm pieces
8. Arrange on a party plate for afternoon tea

Understanding

Shade the bubble for the best answer.

a. All of the points in the method begin with
- ◯ A noun
- ◯ An adjective
- ◯ An adverb
- ◯ A verb

b. Why would you wrap the bread?
- ◯ to keep if firm
- ◯ to do something else
- ◯ to make it easy to cut
- ◯ to leave it for 10 minutes

c. The purpose of this text is to
- ◯ entertain
- ◯ persuade
- ◯ instruct
- ◯ inform

d. A word closer in meaning to method
- ◯ command
- ◯ process
- ◯ manner
- ◯ pattern

Interpreting

Circle **Yes** or **No** to answer each statement

a. These swirls would be suitable for a child's birthday party.	**Yes**	**No**
b. I would be able to make these swirls.	**Yes**	**No**
c. These swirls would look enticing on the plate.	**Yes**	**No**
d. I think this type of fare is new.	**Yes**	**No**
e. These swirls would take a long time to make.	**Yes**	**No**
f. Do you need to cook these swirls?	**Yes**	**No**

Language

Fill in the sentences using an **action verb** from the word bank.

WORD BANK: sprinkle, roll, undo, leave, arrange

a. Cooking often requires time to ______________________ ingredients to settle.

b. Mum often needs to ______________________ mistakes I make in cooking.

c. She was asked to ______________________ the food on the table.

d. Only a ______________________ of salt is needed on our eggs at breakfast.

e. Mum allows me to ______________________ the scone mixture on the board.

Spelling

Look, cover, write, check each word.

slice ______________________ ☐

bread ______________________ ☐

crust ______________________ ☐

sprinkle ______________________ ☐

wrap ______________________ ☐

leave ______________________ ☐

pieces ______________________ ☐

arrange ______________________ ☐

firmly ______________________ ☐

plate ______________________ ☐

Word Building

Use the (adverb) '**off**' and (preposition) '**from**'

It **fell 'off'** the tree. but I got it **'from' the boy.**

Fill in the spaces using '**off**' OR '**from**'

a. It was discovered __________ shore.

b. Pull it __________ me please.

c. They ran __________ danger.

d. He got it __________ his dad.

e. They all moved __________ the spot.

f. The electricity was turned __________ .

g. Now go and get it __________ home.

h. __________ where did he come?

Sentences

Study this sentence: We are coming (**main clause**) before we have tea. (**dependent clause**)
Underline the **dependent** clause in each sentence and **write** the **main clause** on the line.

a. When the rains come, we will be happy. ______________________

b. In the winter, everybody feels cold. ______________________

c. With great haste, they ran for cover. ______________________

d. Which one is ripe, because it looks green? ______________________

e. Last evening, the concert started early. ______________________

Data and Graphs

Here is a graph for rainfall in February. Use the data in the graph to complete the activities.

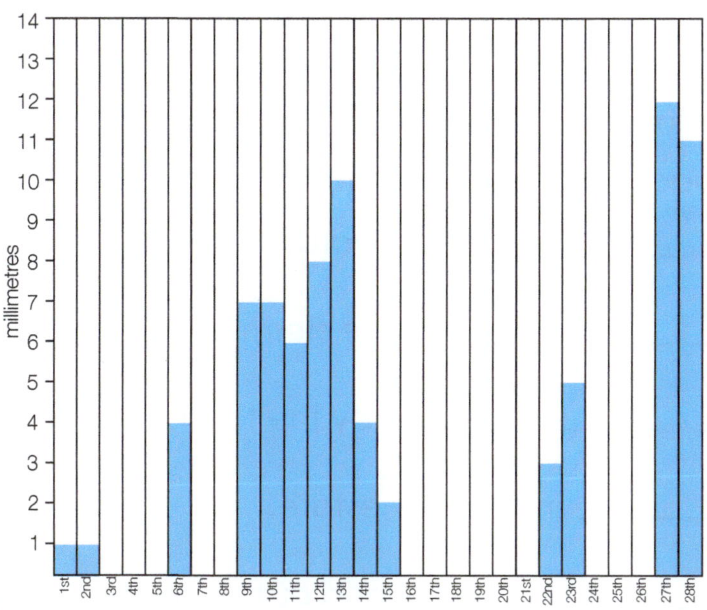

1. How many days without rain? __________

2. On what days were there 4mm of rain?

__________ __________

3. What was the total rainfall between 9 and 15 February? __________ mm

4. What length of time was the driest spell of weather? __________

5. How many rainy days in the month? __________

6. On what day did 6mm of rain fall? __________

7. On which date was the heaviest fall of rain? __________

8. What was the total rainfall for the month? __________

9. Is the month showing a leap year? __________

10. What total is showing in each tally?

a. 𝍸 𝍸 || ______ **b.** 𝍸 𝍸 𝍸 || ______

An Acrostic Poem

The eruption happened at night
Soon the waves roared inland
Until the beach had disappeared
Now all the people panicked
After the water crept back to the sea
Many raced to higher ground
In the hope of surviving

Use this to write your own poem.

T ____________________

S ____________________

U ____________________

N ____________________

A ____________________

M ____________________

I ____________________

Understanding
Shade the bubble for the best answer

a. The 'waves roared' is an example of
- ◯ metaphor
- ◯ personification
- ◯ onomatapaea
- ◯ alliteration

b. Another word for 'eruption' could be
- ◯ disruption
- ◯ accident
- ◯ problem
- ◯ explosion

c. An example of 'alliteration' is
- ◯ waves roared
- ◯ crept back
- ◯ people panicked
- ◯ higher ground

d. The meaning of 'tsunami' is
- ◯ a great wave
- ◯ water spout
- ◯ Japanese fish
- ◯ disappearing beach

Interpreting
Circle **Yes** or **No** to answer each statement

a. Did the tsunami happen in the morning?	**Yes**	**No**
b. Were the people frightened?	**Yes**	**No**
c. Was this a natural disaster?	**Yes**	**No**
d. Did the water swallow the beach?	**Yes**	**No**
e. Can people out-run a tsunami?	**Yes**	**No**
f. Would the beach be a safe place to be?	**Yes**	**No**

Language
Use an **adverb** from the word bank to tell **how, when, where** or **why** about the verb.

WORD BANK: nearby, yesterday, backwards, violently, because

a. The race was run ____________________ by the stewards.

b. The windows shook ____________________ in the storm.

c. The suits were sewn ____________________ by the tailor.

d. Everyone lives ____________________ in the new estate.

e. The young child cried ____________________ he fell and cut his knee.

Spelling

Look, cover, write, check each word.

- erupt ______ ☐
- happen ______ ☐
- waves ______ ☐
- until ______ ☐
- disappear ______ ☐
- panic ______ ☐
- survive ______ ☐
- tsunami ______ ☐
- acrostic ______ ☐
- crept ______ ☐

Word Building

Match a list word to its meaning

a. sneak ______

b. ripple ______

c. vanish ______

d. live ______

e. fear ______

f. blow up ______

Write the **three syllable** list words, in syllables

g. ______

h. ______

i. ______

Sentences

Write the best **conjunction (and, but OR so)**, on the line, to join the sentence.

a. There was no football practice today. We went to the park instead. ______

b. Go to the shop for me. Buy me some fruit and salad. ______

c. We waited for the school bus. It did not come. ______

d. A huge fire broke out at the shop. It was closed to the public. ______

e. It was raining. The class had sport. ______

Mass

1. Write kilograms (kg) or grams (g) as the unit of mass for each object.

a.

75 ______

b.

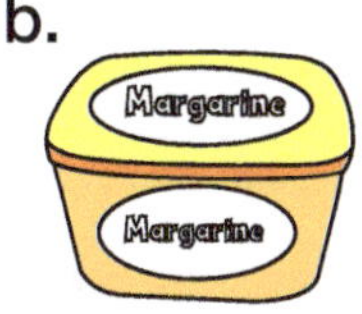

500 ______

c.

75 ______

2. Write each mass in its shortest form: kg or g

a. 80 kilograms ______ **b.** 60 grams ______

c. 1 1/2 kilograms ______ **d.** 500 grams ______

e. 2000 kilograms ______ **f.** 250 grams ______

g. 2500 kilograms ______ **h.** 700 grams ______

i. 250 kilograms ______ **j.** 25 grams ______

Square Centimetre

1. Count the square centimetres in each shape.

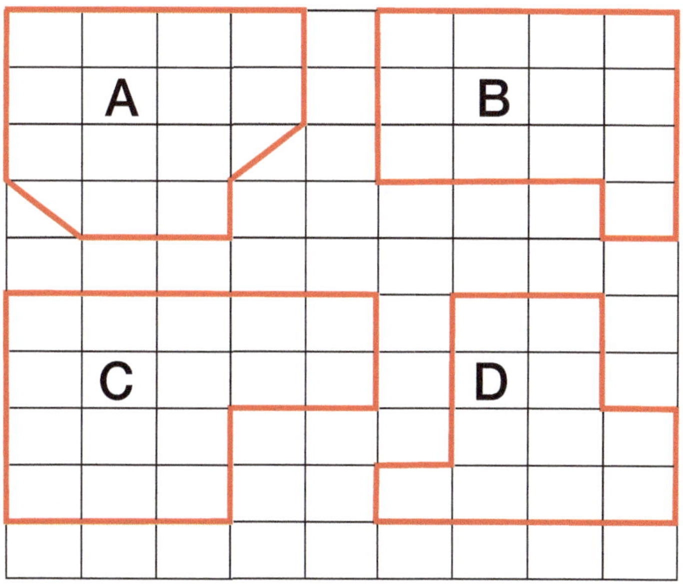

2. Which shape is the biggest? ______

The Sydney Opera House

This amazing building was designed by a Danish architect called Jørn Utzon. It is built on Bennelong Point in Sydney Harbour and took many years to build. Work commenced in 1957 but it wasn't opened until 1973 by Queen Elizabeth II.

Seven tiled shells or 'sails' make up the roof of the Opera House. They are called 'sails' because they look like unfurled sails on those first ships that entered Sydney Harbour in 1788. These shells lock into one another and have a 100 metre wide stairway leading up to them from the forecourt.

Inside the building there are walls of glass, timber-lined halls and huge concrete beams. There are two large concert halls, side by side, designed for use by many different performing arts. Not only opera is performed in this opera house. Ballet, Pop Concerts, Ceremonies and even State Funerals have been held in the Sydney Opera House.

In 2013 the Danish Royal Family attended the 40th anniversary of the opening of the Sydney Opera House. This was to honour the architect's nationality as well as celebrate this beautiful building in Australia.

Understanding

Tick the box if the information is in the text

a. The Sydney Opera House designer was Dutch. ☐
b. It is 40 years old. ☐
c. It took nearly twenty years to build. ☐
d. It is only used for opera. ☐
e. There are nine shells on its roof. ☐
f. Its walls are made of glass. ☐
g. Queen Elizabeth II opened it. ☐
h. There are seven halls inside. ☐
i. It has many uses. ☐
j. State Funerals are held there. ☐

Interpreting

Write an answer to each question.

a. Where is the Sydney Opera House? ____________________

b. Name a performing art you might see at the Opera House. ____________________

c. Who celebrated its fortieth anniversary? ____________________

d. What is a State Funeral? ____________________

e. Where is Bennelong Point ? ____________________

Language

Abbreviated words with apostrophes are contractions. Write the shortened word in these,

a. they're ____________________ **b.** weren't ____________________

c. he's ____________________ **d.** you'll ____________________

e. I'm ____________________ **f.** you've ____________________

g. I'd ____________________ **h.** who's ____________________

i. can't ____________________ **j.** it'll ____________________

Spelling

Look, cover, write, check each word.

- architect ______________ ☐
- commenced ______________ ☐
- unfurled ______________ ☐
- entered ______________ ☐
- concrete ______________ ☐
- concert ______________ ☐
- performance ______________ ☐
- celebrate ______________ ☐
- honour ______________ ☐
- beautiful ______________ ☐

Word Building

Learn these **contracted** words.

its	**but**	it's = it is,
your	**but**	you're = you are
whose	**but**	who's = who is
their	**but**	they're = they are
his	**but**	he's = he is

Other **possessive pronouns** to watch

ours, yours, hers, theirs,

It is **ours** but that is **yours**. This is **hers**.

That is **theirs** and **they're** not having it.

Whose pen is on **your** desk?

Sentences

Use these **possessives** correctly in a sentence.

they're theirs their they he's his you're yours who's whose

a. Did you see ______________ new skateboard that ______________ bought?

b. ______________ not going to have any because ______________ is at home.

c. That was ______________ but now ______________ not taking it with them.

d. Do you know ______________ coming and ______________ not?

e. ______________ turn is it to make lunch?

Money

1. Round off each price to the nearest five cents.

a. $8.32 __________ **b.** $23.84 __________

c. $9.57 __________ **d.** $105.21 __________

e. $68.39 __________ **f.** $55.83 __________

2. Write the number of coins needed to equal each note.

a.  is equal to ☐ 50 cents

b.  is equal to ☐ $2 coins

c.  is equal to ☐ 50 cents

d.  is equal to ☐ $2 coins

Symmetry

1. Shapes without symmetry are called '**asymmetrical**' shapes. Colour the '**asymmetrical**' shapes.

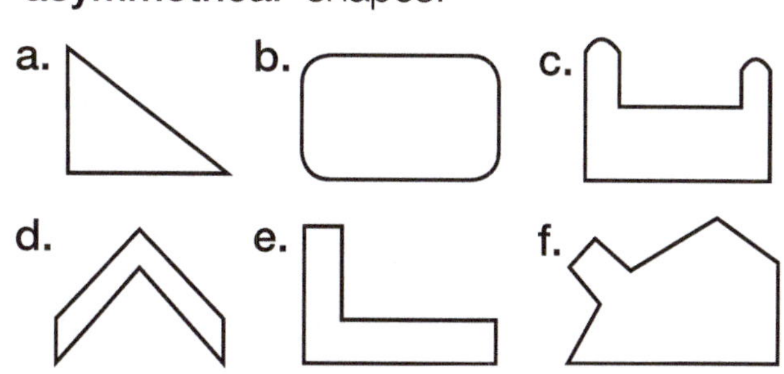

2. Use different colours to highlight this pattern.

School Students Should Wear a Uniform

I agree with this statement most of the time, but there are some times when I disagree too. I will explain my reasons for you.

School uniforms have been worn by students all around the country for a very long time. There are some schools where the uniform is so well recognised that it is seen as a 'badge of honour' to wear it. One might say that the uniform shapes the character of the person wearing it. It can be used to identify the person's pride in how they look by how it is worn. A uniform recognises belonging to a group that has like-minded attitudes and values. It marks one's awareness of a school membership and creates an expected behaviour when it is worn. Therefore, I think wearing a school uniform is important for building community and character.

On the other hand, if the expense is prohibitive, then it may not be possible for all children to wear a school uniform. If this is the case maybe the school should accommodate these students. Exceptions could be made when students are unable to wear the uniform and not just say that it must be worn at all times. There needs to be some consideration given to help those who are unable to always wear a uniform.

So while I can see merit in wearing a school uniform I am also aware that it is not always possible for all students to wear one.

Understanding

Shade the bubble for the best answer

a. What is the meaning of 'badge of honour'?
- ◯ something that shines
- ◯ a worthwhile person
- ◯ a distinguishing brooch
- ◯ a token of respect

b. Why is a school uniform important?
- ◯ to show belonging
- ◯ for building honour
- ◯ as a mark of respect
- ◯ to look alike

c. What does 'prohibitive' mean?
- ◯ within reach
- ◯ out of reach
- ◯ too much
- ◯ not much

d. What is the main purpose of this text?
- ◯ to provide an answer
- ◯ to argue a point of view
- ◯ to decide on a school uniform
- ◯ to argue two points of view

Interpreting

Tick the box if the information is in the text

a. It is important to wear a school uniform. ☐
b. School uniforms are distinguishing clothes. ☐
c. School uniforms show one belongs to a group. ☐
d. A school uniform shapes a person's character. ☐
e. School uniforms are too expensive for some parents. ☐

Language

Use the **persuasive language** in the Word bank, to fill in the blanks

WORD BANK: I agree, on the other hand, should, if, I think, would

Mary and her sister ______________ be able to attend our party. However, ______________

that it may be too far to come. ________ , ______________________________ , their mum

could bring them, that ____________________ be great!

Spelling

Unit 8

Look, cover, write, check each word.

- statement ______________ ☐
- disagree ______________ ☐
- uniform ______________ ☐
- recognise ______________ ☐
- character ______________ ☐
- identify ______________ ☐
- aware ______________ ☐
- behaviour ______________ ☐
- accommodate ______________ ☐
- consider ______________ ☐

Word Building

List words with **suffixes** - 'tion', 'ment', 'ness'
Write each word, in **syllables**.

a. accommodation ______________

b. consideration ______________

c. recognition ______________

d. identification ______________

e. formation ______________

f. disagreement ______________

g. awareness ______________

h. statement ______________

i. recognising ______________

j. characterisation ______________

Sentences

Write on the line **all** the **personal pronouns** in each sentence.

a. I agree with you but will he agree with me? ______________

b. You are going to school and I am going to her place for lunch. ______________

c. Their books were missing when she and her sister went to the library ______________

d. That bag is yours, this is hers and that belongs to his mother. ______________

e. This is mine and that is yours but they are ours. ______________

Length

1. Measure the length of each line to the nearest centimetre.

a. ______________________

______ cm

b. ________________

______ cm

c. __________________________

______ cm

2. Use a ruler and draw lines of these lengths.

a. 4cm
•

b. 6cm
•

c. 7½cm
•

Temperature

Use thermometers to answer the questions.

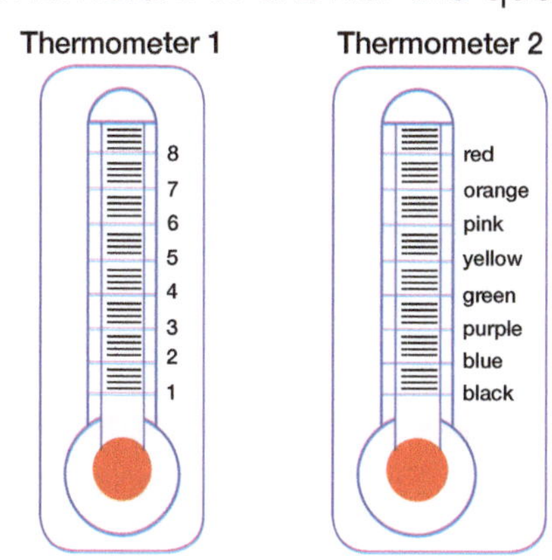

1. If the temperature on thermometer 1 shows **6**, what would thermometer 2 show? ______________

2. If thermometer 2 shows a reading of blue, what would thermometer 1 show? ______________

A Cheap Night Out

Here is the menu board at the local café.

ADULTS		KIDS' SPECIALS	
Fish and Chips	$10.00	Nuggets and Chips	$ 5.00
Chicken Schnitzel	$12.00	Fish Fingers and Chips	$ 5.00
Salt and Pepper Squid	$12.00	Salad and Chips	$ 5.00
Rissoles and gravy	$10.00	Fried Rice	$ 4.00
Sausages and Mash	$8.00	Chips and Gravy	$ 3.50
Lasagne	$9.00	Ice Cream with Syrup	$ 2.50

Kids half price when accompanied with an adult

Understanding Circle **Yes** or **No** for your answer.

a.	Does the café have a large range of food for sale?	**Yes**	**No**
b.	Would you like to eat at this café?	**Yes**	**No**
c.	Does this café encourage adults with kids?	**Yes**	**No**
d.	Do you often eat out?	**Yes**	**No**
e.	Could you afford to eat at this café?	**Yes**	**No**

Interpreting Write an answer to each question.

a. What is the cheapest food on the adults' menu? ______________________

b. How much would it cost for your mum to eat fish and chips at the café? ______________________

c. How much would it cost you to eat the same meal with her? ______________________

d. Why are there "Kids' Specials" ? ______________________

e. What is the meaning of 'mash'? ______________________

Language Underline the adjectival clauses in each sentence. The first one is done for you.

a. The house, which Jack built, is blue.

b. The boy, who ran down the road, was Jon.

c. The house where Paris lived, is there.

d. Purple is the colour that I like best.

e. Tell me whose jacket was stolen.

f. The man, to whom I am reading, is blind.

g. The sign, which was broken, fell off.

h. Many people, who went missing, were boys.

Spelling

Look, cover, write, check each word.

menu ______________ ☐

cheap ______________ ☐

chicken ______________ ☐

squid ______________ ☐

gravy ______________ ☐

sausage ______________ ☐

local ______________ ☐

adult ______________ ☐

rissole ______________ ☐

accompany ______________ ☐

Word Building

Compound Words - Write each one as two words.

a. homework ________ ________

b. something ________ ________

c. anywhere ________ ________

d. sometimes ________ ________

e. daybreak ________ ________

f. sunshine ________ ________

g. bedroom ________ ________

h. teacup ________ ________

i. wheelbarrow ________ ________

j. blackmail ________ ________

Sentences

Re-write each sentence using **commas** where needed.

a. The boy who was sick had books pens pencils and toys to use.

____

b. The shoes which were the wrong size were returned for a refund.

____

c. Red, purple, green and blue are colours that I like best.

____

Multiplying by 6

1. Complete this table of multiplication by 6.

a. 6 x 0 = ☐ **b.** 6 x 5 = ☐

c. 6 x 1 = ☐ **d.** 6 x 6 = ☐

e. 6 x 2 = ☐ **f.** 6 x 7 = ☐

g. 6 x 3 = ☐ **h.** 6 x 8 = ☐

i. 6 x 4 = ☐ **j.** 6 x 9 = ☐

2. Complete this number wheel.

start here

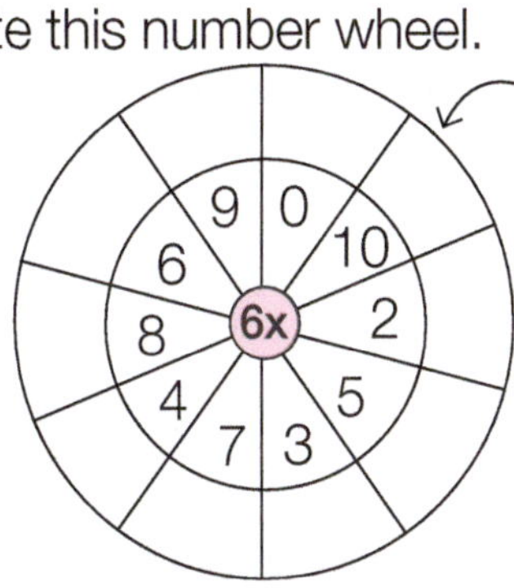

Multiplying by 7, 8 and 9

a. 6 x 7 = ☐ **b.** 4 x 8 = ☐

c. 8 x 5 = ☐ **d.** 9 x 3 = ☐

e. 7 x 7 = ☐ **f.** 8 x 8 = ☐

g. 9 x 6 = ☐ **h.** 8 x 7 = ☐

2. Complete this number wheel.

start here

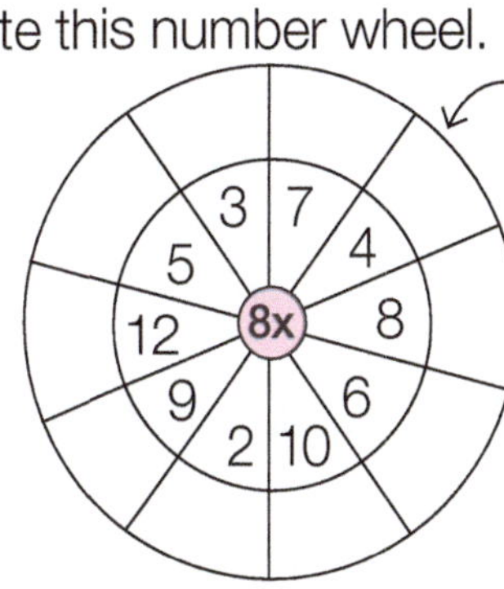

Gold and the Eureka Rebellion

At the beginning of the 1850s Victoria experienced an influx of people, particularly Chinese, who came to Australia to explore for gold.

When gold was discovered in 1851, word soon spread so people flocked to places like Ballarat and Bendigo, Castlemaine and the surrounding hills to dig for gold. These towns began to prosper.

However, the government wanted to share in the wealth, so in 1854 it imposed a licence fee, to be paid, by the miners, one month in advance. Because the miners thought this was unfair, they rebelled and refused to pay. Some even burnt their licence in defiance. This rebellion was about the right of ordinary people to have a vote and a say, in how they were governed.

The rebellion became known as the Eureka Rebellion; 'eureka' being the cry given by a miner when he struck it rich and discovered gold. Their leader was Peter Lalor and he was later elected to Parliament.

With the new-found wealth of the miners came a new style of living. Ornate buildings, some of which are still standing today, added to the beauty of these towns.

Understanding

Write an answer to each question

a. In what Australian state was gold first discovered? __________

b. What nationality were some early miners of gold in Australia? __________

c. Who wanted to share the miners' wealth? __________

d. What act of defiance did the miners commit? __________

e. What was the name of the rebellion? __________

Interpreting

Shade the bubble for the best answer

a. Another word for 'influx' is
- ◯ hurry ◯ rush
- ◯ storm ◯ attack

b. The word 'eureka' means
- ◯ joyful ◯ great
- ◯ lost it ◯ found it

c. What was this 'new-found' wealth?
- ◯ silver ◯ self-government
- ◯ gold ◯ the vote

d. Choose another word for 'ornate'
- ◯ ornament ◯ decorative
- ◯ pretty ◯ stylish

Language

Underline the **adverbial phrase** in each sentence.

a. At the beginning, miners worked hard.

b. Now and then, they had a rest.

c. Word spread, around the camp.

d. The miners rebelled, before long.

e. They rebelled, for their rights.

f. Ornate buildings, in Bendigo, still stand.

Spelling

Look, cover, write, check each word.

beginning ______________ ☐

influx ______________ ☐

discover ______________ ☐

spread ______________ ☐

aprosper ______________ ☐

wealth ______________ ☐

advance ______________ ☐

licence ______________ ☐

ordinary ______________ ☐

ornate ______________ ☐

Word Building

Homophones - Write the meaning
Use your **dictionary**

a. licence (n) ______________

b. license (v) ______________

c. stationery (n) ______________

d. stationary (adj) ______________

e. dependant (n) ______________

f. dependent (adj) ______________

g. principle (n) ______________

h. principal (adj) ______________

i. practice (n) ______________

j. practise (v) ______________

Sentences

Complete each sentence using the correct **proper noun**.

Sydney Darwin Hobart Adelaide Brisbane

a. The capital city of Tasmania is ______________ .

b. In New South Wales the capital is ______________ .

c. Northern Territory's capital city is ______________ .

d. The capital city of South Australia is ______________ .

e. However, ______________ is the capital of Queensland.

Capacity

1. Write Litres (L) or millilitres (mL) as the unit of capacity for each container.

a. 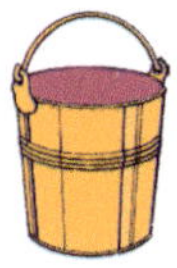

11 _____

b. 

250 _____

c. 

2 _____

2. Record the water level in this container in millilitres.

Volume = _____ mL

3. Write each millilitre in litres and millilitres.

a. 1 250 mL = _____ L _____ mL

b. 22 550 mL = _____ L _____ mL

Location

1. Label the cardinal points on each directional rose. Show north **N**, south **S**, east **E**, west **W**.

N

a. 

b. 

N

2. In which direction will I travel for -

a. X to Z **b.** Z to Y

c. Y to ∞ **d.** ∞ to A

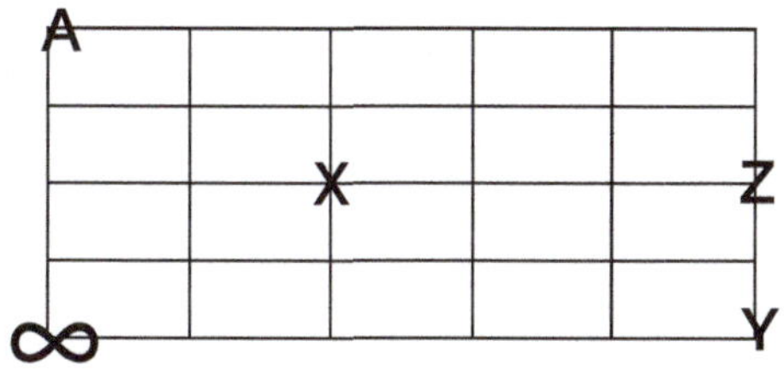

a. _____

b. _____

c. _____

d. _____

The Platypus

The platypus is another warm-blooded animal, or monotreme that lays eggs and the mother produces milk to feed her young, just like the echidna. It is one of only two egg-laying mammals in the World.

All mammals have a back-bone and some grow fur on their bodies to keep warm. The platypus has fur on its body and is unique in that it is part-reptile and part-mammal, with a duck-bill and webbed feet.

The female platypus lays her eggs in a deep burrow on the side of a muddy river bank or stream. She hatches them with her warm, furry body and then feeds her young on her milk.

The other monotreme is the echidna and both animals are native to Australia. They are found nowhere else in the World.

Understanding

Tick the box if the information is in the text

a. The platypus is like the echidna. ☐

b. Female platypus have milk. ☐

c. The platypus is a monotreme. ☐

d. You will find platypus in water. ☐

e. Platypus burrows are found on land. ☐

f. The platypus is a reptile. ☐

g. A platypus is found anywhere. ☐

h. The platypus only lays two eggs. ☐

i. Platypus grows fur on its body. ☐

j. It hatches its young in the water. ☐

Interpreting

Match a word to its meaning

WORD BANK: back-bone flat-footed reptile mammal webbed-feet hatches

a. platypus ____________

b. cold-blooded ____________

c. warm blooded ____________

d. membrane covering digits ____________

e. spine or vertebra ____________

f. incubates ____________

Language

Circle the **adjectives** and underline the **nouns** in each sentence.

a. The platypus is a warm-blooded animal or monotreme.

b. It is only one of two egg-laying mammals in the World.

c. The female platypus feeds her young on her milk.

d. The other monotreme is the echidna and both are found in Australia.

e. All mammals have a back-bone and some grow fur on their bodies.

Spelling

Look, cover, write, check each word.

another ______ ☐
bodies ______ ☐
grow ______ ☐
unique ______ ☐
reptile ______ ☐
webbed ______ ☐
burrow ______ ☐
hatches ______ ☐
monotreme ______ ☐
World ______ ☐

Word Building

Write the meaning of each word

a. mammal ______

______

b. marsupial ______

______

c. monotreme ______

______

Sentences

Underline the **how and when (adverbial) phrases** in each sentence.

a. They ran quickly down the street.

b. We cooked in the afternoon.

c. I am going on the bus, this afternoon.

d. She had dinner before the concert.

e. Slowly but surely, the tortoise finished.

f. Now and then we play after dinner.

Decimal Fractions

1. Write a decimal fraction for each of these.

a. $\frac{1}{2}$ = ___ **b.** $\frac{1}{4}$ = ___ **c.** $\frac{1}{10}$ = ___

d. $\frac{1}{5}$ = ___ **e.** $\frac{4}{10}$ = ___ **f.** $\frac{4}{5}$ = ___

g. $\frac{3}{4}$ = ___ **h.** $\frac{3}{10}$ = ___ **i.** $\frac{3}{5}$ = ___

2. Write each decimal as a fraction.

a. 0.5 = ______ **b.** 0.2 = ______

c. 0.7 = ______ **d.** 0.25 = ______

e. 0.1 = ______ **f.** 0.4 = ______

g. 2.9 = ______ **h.** 1.75 = ______

3. Arrange this set of fractions in **ascending** order.

0.3, $\frac{1}{4}$, 0.7, $\frac{1}{2}$, 0.2

______ ______ ______ ______ ______

Factors and Multiplies

1. Write the multiple of each set of factors.

a. 6 x 4 = ☐ **b.** 7 x 3 = ☐

c. 9 x 10 = ☐ **d.** 6 x 8 = ☐

e. 7 x 8 = ☐ **f.** 9 x 5 = ☐

g. 3 x 9 = ☐ **h.** 4 x 9 = ☐

2. Write factors for each number.

4 ______

7 ______

5 ______

3 ______

3. Write (T) true or (F) false for each statement.

a. 2 x 3 = 3 x 2 ______

b. 18 is a multiple of 3 ______

c. 48 is a multiple of 6 ______

Skateboards should be Banned

In my opinion skateboards are good when used in a special skate park but when used on the road or footpath then I agree, they should be banned.

First of all a skateboard is dangerous when used on the road because the rider can fall off and be run over. Or, on the other hand, a rider could cause a driver to have a serious accident. This could lead to the rider, the driver and even passengers being seriously injured or killed.

Then there is a danger to a skateboarder which can be long-lasting. Broken arms, legs, wrists and serious knee injuries are known to happen but worst of all a severe head injury can have very serious and long-lasting consequences.

As well as these reasons there is a danger to the elderly when skateboards are used on a footpath. Elderly people can't move very quickly, nor are they expecting to have to get out of the way of a fast-moving skateboard rider.

So as you can see, I believe skateboards should be banned if they are used in places other than a specially designated skate park.

Understanding

Circle **Yes** or **No** to answer each statement

a. Skateboards should always be used in a skate park. **Yes** **No**

b. Young people are the only ones who skate. **Yes** **No**

c. It is dangerous to skate on the footpath. **Yes** **No**

d. Skateboards cause serious injury. **Yes** **No**

e. Car drivers can be killed by skateboard riders. **Yes** **No**

Interpreting

Write an answer to each question

a. Why is it dangerous to skate on a footpath? ______________________________

____

b. What are some injuries you can receive if you ride a skateboard? ______________________________

____

Language

Underline the best word in brackets **to argue strongly** your point of view.

a. I (might, will) go to school today.

b. You (could, should) look before you leap.

c. (Certainly, maybe) I shall find it.

d. How far (can, must) you go to win?

e. You will win (if, because) you are fast.

f. (I believe, I know) it is raining outside.

Spelling

Look, cover, write, check each word.

- dangerous ______________ ☐
- serious ______________ ☐
- accident ______________ ☐
- passenger ______________ ☐
- injuries ______________ ☐
- severe ______________ ☐
- consequence ______________ ☐
- elderly ______________ ☐
- designated ______________ ☐
- opinion ______________ ☐

Word Building

When using the **prefix** '**all**' drop one 'l'

Write these two words as one word

a. all so ______________

b. all together ______________

c. all though ______________

d. all ways ______________

e. all most ______________

f. all mighty ______________

g. all ready ______________

An exception to the rule is **all right**

Sentences

Use these **prepositions**, to begin the **adverbial phrases**, correctly.

WORD BANK: on to after before in until

a. We ran ______________ it was dark.

b. Put the book ______________ the table.

c. ______________ long, we will go home.

d. He ran ______________ the ball but lost it.

e. _____ the morning, we will have breakfast.

f. We went ______________ the park to play.

Primes and Multiples

A prime number has only one set of factors - itself and one. It can only be divided by itself and one.

1. Circle the prime numbers in this array.

1	2	3	4	5	6	7
8	9	10	11	12	13	14
15	16	17	18	19	20	21

2. Colour the multiples of 4.

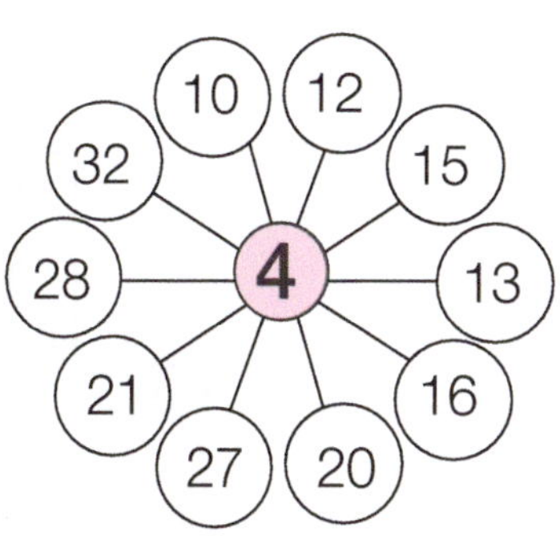

Division

1. Complete each division sentence.

a. 54 ÷ 6 = ☐

b. 32 ÷ 8 = ☐

c. 39 ÷ 3 = ☐

d. 42 ÷ 7 = ☐

e. 63 ÷ 9 = ☐

f. 64 ÷ 8 = ☐

g. 100 ÷ 2 = ☐

h. 99 ÷ 3 = ☐

2. Divide by six or three.

a. 42 ÷ 6 = ☐

b. 30 ÷ 3 = ☐

c. 24 ÷ 6 = ☐

d. 24 ÷ 3 = ☐

e. 18 ÷ 6 = ☐

f. 27 ÷ 3 = ☐

g. 36 ÷ 6 = ☐

h. 42 ÷ 3 = ☐

More International Space Travel

Unit 3 in this book, covers space travel up to and including 1969.

1970 America's Apollo 13 suffered an explosion in orbit but NASA scientists on board repaired the damage and brought the spaceship safely back to Earth.

1971 The Moon car known as the Lunar Rover was used by Apollo 4, 5 and 6 astronauts to explore the surface of the Moon.

1973 Mars 2, built in 2 sections, was to be used by Russia to explore the surface of Mars. However, the parachute on one probe failed to open and it was destroyed.

1986 Tragedy struck Space Shuttle Challenger shortly after lift-off due to a fuel system failure. All seven astronauts on board were killed. Shuttles were then grounded for three years. This same year the Russian MIR space station was started and it took ten years to build. (MIR is "peace" or "World" in Russian)

1991 The first British astronaut took part in a Russian mission to the MIR space station.

2000 The first permanent crews moved into the International Space Station (ISS). Crews of astronauts and cosmonauts have been living in the ISS ever since.

2020 It is expected that America will be back at the Moon and set up a permanent moon-base there.

Understanding
Write the date for each event

a. Tragedy struck the space mission. ________ **b.** The Lunar Rover was used by Apollo 4 ________

c. Astronauts live in space. ________ **d.** Building of the MIR space station began. ________

e. Apollo 13 was repaired in space. ________ **f.** Lunar Rover explored the moon's surface. ________

g. Seven astronauts were killed. ________ **h.** One section of Mars 2 was destroyed. ________

i. Permanent crews moved into the ISS. ________ **j.** America hopes to set up a moon-base. ________

Interpreting
Match a word to its meaning

WORD BANK: : lunar historical exploration permanent shuttle explosion

a. lasting, with no time limit ____________ **b.** relating to the moon ____________

c. dealing with past events ____________ **d.** to expand with force ____________

e. going back and forth ____________ **f.** moving for purpose of discovery ____________

Language
Here is a list of **acronyms**. Match them to their meanings.

ISS UN ISBN NSW

a. International Space Station ________________

b. New South Wales ________________

c. United Nation ________________

d. International Standard Book Number ________________

Spelling

Look, cover, write, check each word.

historical ______________ ☐
expert ______________ ☐
explore ______________ ☐
explode ______________ ☐
experiment ______________ ☐
parachute ______________ ☐
tragedy ______________ ☐
astronaut ______________ ☐
permanent ______________ ☐
damage ______________ ☐

Word Building

Nouns ending in s, x, z, sh & ch add "es" for plural

bus ______________ box ______________
buzz ______________ bush ______________
church ______________ fox ______________
kiss ______________ wish ______________
lurch ______________ hush ______________

Form **past tense** by adding "ed"

explode ______________
experiment ______________
explore ______________

Sentences

Write the two words that form each **contraction**.

a. didn't ______________ **b.** shan't ______________
c. you're ______________ **d.** they'll ______________
e. they're ______________ **f.** he's ______________

Place Value

1. Write the number showing in each place value frame.

a.

TTH	TH	H	T	O
II	IIII	I		IIII

____

b.

TTH	TH	H	T	O
IIIIII	II		III	IIIII

____

c.

TTH	TH	H	T	O
I		IIII	I	III

____

d.

TTH	TH	H	T	O
IIIII		III	I	II

____

2. Here are sums of money. The decimal point separates the cents from dollars. Identify the place value of circled numerals as thousands, hundreds, tens and ones.

a. $1③6.70 ______________
b. $③754.30 ______________
c. $214⑤.60 ______________
d. $⑦29.75 ______________

Decimal Fractions

1. Write the fraction showing on the hundredth frame.

a.
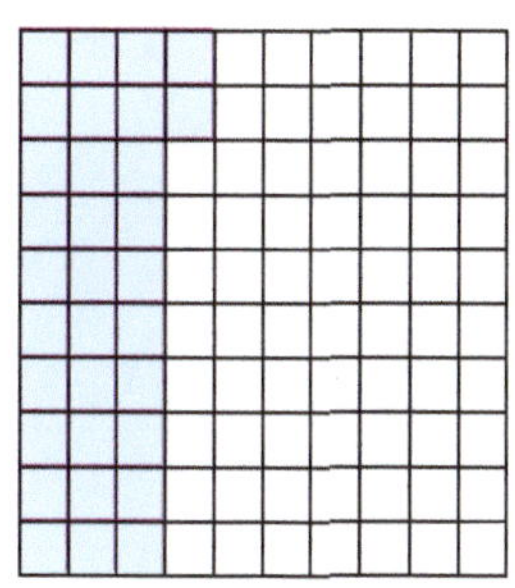
0.______________

b.
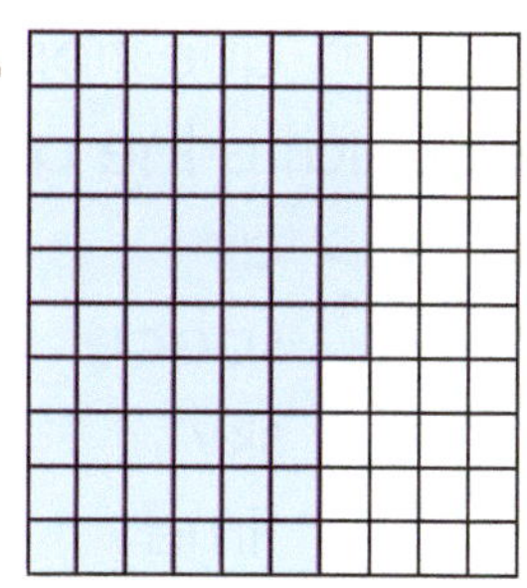
0.______________

2. Each frame shows a whole number and a decimal fraction. Write the number.

a.

TH	H	T	O	Tths	Hdths
III	II	III	II •	IIIIII	IIII

____

b.

TH	H	T	O	Tths	Hdths
IIIIII		IIII	II •	IIIII	IIIIII

____

c.

TH	H	T	O	Tths	Hdths
I	III	IIII	II •	I	IIIII

____

Why is the Sky Blue?

Have you ever wondered about the phenomenon - why the sky is blue?

The sky has no colour of its own. It only reflects the colour blue from all the particles that pass through the sun.

The sunlight, which contains all the colours, passes through the atmosphere and scatters millions of particles through the air. These particles reflect the colour blue which is the strongest of colours in the sunlight. Therefore, the sky appears to be blue.

Where Does Sand Come From?

This is another puzzle to most of us.

Sand is made up of small particles of mineral substances like silica and quartz. But where do these come from to make sand?

The constant movement of the water, crashing against the shore line, breaks down the rock containing these substances. Then it falls into the ocean and is washed up on beaches as sand.

Understanding

Shade the bubble for the best answer

a. This information
- ◯ describes
- ◯ informs
- ◯ explains
- ◯ instructs

b. Why is the sky blue?
- ◯ blue is in the sunlight
- ◯ blue is a strong colour
- ◯ blue is in the atmosphere
- ◯ blue is reflected through the sun

c. What does 'phenomena' mean?
- ◯ strange
- ◯ strong
- ◯ event
- ◯ question

d. What minerals are in sand?
- ◯ silver and quartz
- ◯ quartz and silica
- ◯ silica and silver
- ◯ rock and sand

e. What is the atmosphere?
- ◯ air
- ◯ space
- ◯ sky
- ◯ time

f. How is sand formed?
- ◯ by crushing
- ◯ by erosion
- ◯ by blasting
- ◯ by cutting

Interpreting

Write an answer to each question

a. Where is the shoreline? ______________________

b. How long does it take for sand to form? ______________________

c. Where is the atmosphere? ______________________

d. What makes a beach? ______________________

Language

Underline the **technical language** in each sentence.

a. Silica and quartz are the main minerals found in sand.

b. Colours in sunlight pass through the atmosphere and scatter particles through the air.

Spelling

Look, cover, write, check each word.

wondered ______ ☐
colour ______ ☐
through ______ ☐
particles ______ ☐
contain ______ ☐
atmosphere ______ ☐
reflect ______ ☐
mineral ______ ☐
silica ______ ☐
quartz ______ ☐

Word Building

Syllabification - write each word in syllables

a. atmosphere ______
b. containing ______
c. particles ______
d. substances ______
e. phenomena ______
f. explanation ______

Unjumble each word -

g. phmostaere ______
h. phmennoea ______
i. phphogotra ______

Sentences

Re-write each sentence using correct **punctuation**.

a. hes going to buy the game of thrones

______

b. its too late now so well miss our turn on the game

______

c. why didnt your parents have toms dinner ready

______

d. he shouldve gone to school for today

______

Multiplication

1. Complete each with even number products.

a. 6 x 4 = ☐ **b.** 8 x 2 = ☐
c. 4 x 8 = ☐ **d.** 10 x 6 = ☐
e. 2 x 4 = ☐ **f.** 6 x 8 = ☐
g. 10 x 8 = ☐ **h.** 2 x 6 = ☐

Addition

1. Add these. There is a need for re-grouping in the ones column.

a.

	Th	H	T	O
	3	2	6	5
+	3	4	1	7

b.

	Th	H	T	O
	6	5	6	8
+	2	1	2	2

Division

1. Complete each simple division and its related multiplication.

a. 3)27 ; 27 ÷ 3 = ☐ ; 3 x 9 = ☐
b. 4)32 ; 32 ÷ 4 = ☐ ; 4 x 8 = ☐
c. 6)54 ; 54 ÷ 6 = ☐ ; 6 x 9 = ☐
d. 7)63 ; 63 ÷ 7 = ☐ ; 7 x 9 = ☐

Subtraction

1. Subtract these. There is a need to re-group the ones and tens column.

a.

	Th	H	T	O
	5	6	7	6
−	2	5	2	9

b.

	Th	H	T	O
	7	6	4	3
+	2	2	2	9

Letter to a Pen Friend

15 June 2015

Dear James

I am a ten year old boy living on a farm in North Queensland. I have one sister who is only seven. Our farm is a long way from other farms and there are no other boys my age living nearby. I would really like to have a pen-friend whom I can write to, or even send an email, so I can share the interesting things I do each day with him.

Do you have any brothers or sisters? Where do you live and where do you go to school?

I don't go to school. My mother teaches my sister and me each day and we use School of the Air to help us with our work. It is great fun! Have you ever heard of this? We can join in with other children when we go 'on air' and we all share things about our English and Maths. I like it.

I would really like you to write to me and tell me all about yourself. I have put my address on this letter and also my email address.

From someone wanting to be your pen-friend,
Henry Jones jhenry05@yahoo.com
RMB 5467, Burke Road,
via Cloncurry Qld 4824

Understanding Circle **T** (True) of **F** (False) to answer correctly

a. This letter was sent by Email.	**T**	**F**	**b.** Henry sent this letter	**T**	**F**
c. James wrote the letter.	**T**	**F**	**d.** James has a pen-friend	**T**	**F**
e. Henry lives in town	**T**	**F**	**f.** The writer goes to school	**T**	**F**
g. James has one brother	**T**	**F**	**h.** Henry has one brother	**T**	**F**
i. Cloncurry is in Queensland	**T**	**F**	**k.** School of the Air is fun	**T**	**F**

Interpreting Write an answer to each question

a. Why did Henry include his Email address? ____________________

____

b. Who would make the best pen-friend for Henry? Explain your reason. ____________________

____

c. What has Henry asked James to do? ____________________

____

Language Write the **noun** using the **apostrophe** correctly to **show possession**.

a. childrens books ____________________ **b.** mums new dress ____________________

c. James bag ____________________ **d.** three friends homes ____________________

Spelling

Look, cover, write, check each word.

- interest ______ ☐
- really ______ ☐
- teaches ______ ☐
- teachers ______ ☐
- heard ______ ☐
- herd ______ ☐
- children ______ ☐
- address ______ ☐
- would ______ ☐
- wood ______ ☐

Word Building

Homophones - match A with B

A	B
a. teaches	**g.** timber
b. teachers	**h.** listen
c. heard	**i.** instructs
d. herd	**k.** instructors
e. would	**l.** group
f. wood	**m.** statement

Edit these. Circle the incorrect words.

Meny peple found the trip to difekult.

Wen the brite lite was on it was gud.

Wud you please sit in the rite seet.

Sentences

Choose the correct word for each space.

WORD BANK: wood teaches herd teachers

a. There is a very large ______ of cows in Mr Smith's dairy.

b. How much ______ will you need to make the drawers?

c. Mrs Thomas ______ us English and Music.

d. All of the ______ are going on the excursion.

Cross Section

1. Draw the shape you see when the 3D object is cut away.

a. 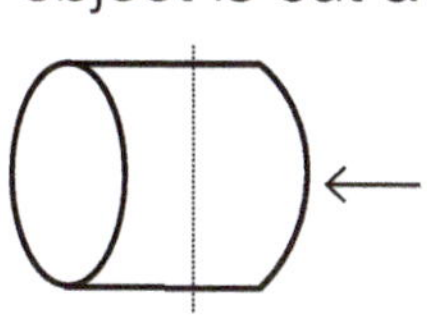

b. 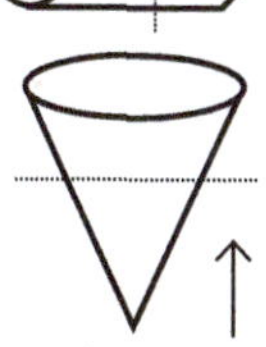

c. 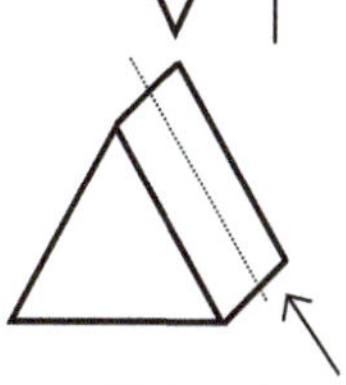

2. Name this shape *(Not arrow)*

______

Lines

1. Match each line to its description or type.

a.		**vertical**
b.		**horizontal**
c.		**oblique**
d.	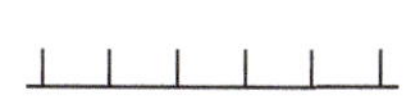	**parallel**
e.		**perpendicular**

2. Make a list of things that have parallel lines, sides or rails.

______

______

Secrets and Spies

Secrets and Spies is a short story written by a group of past Year Four students, as an entry for the Short Story Competition held annually by the Chronicle.

The students have concentrated on building intrigue and suspense into their writing. So you can imagine what to expect, particularly if you like this type of read.

Not only do the characters in *Secrets and Spies* find themselves in places where information is mixed with truth and lies but just how do they separate truth from fiction? There are many opportunities to explore the secrets they uncover but their biggest dilemma is to know when to expose them or just discount them as lies. Perhaps you can decide?

Do be sure to look up this work in your school library and decide for yourself whether it is worthy of winning the Chronicle's prize for the best entry into the competition. Or perhaps you could get together with a group of friends and write such a story yourself.

Understanding

Circle **Yes** or **No** to answer each statement

a. This is a real story.	**Yes**	**No**	**b.** It is in the school library.	**Yes**	**No**
c. My friend wrote the script	**Yes**	**No**	**d.** This is a short story.	**Yes**	**No**
e. It is full of intrigue	**Yes**	**No**	**f.** The Chronicle won a prize	**Yes**	**No**
g. The story is fiction	**Yes**	**No**	**h.** The story is a fable	**Yes**	**No**

Interpreting

Write an answer to each question

a. What is the dilemma facing the characters in *Secrets and Spies*?

____

b. What does the reading suggest you might do?

____

c. In what competition was the story entered?

____

d. What do you think the Chronicle is?

____

Language

Adjectives add meaning to nouns. Write the adjective or adjectives in each sentence on the line.

a. Here is a short story written by past Year 4 students. ______________

b. It won the short story Competition. ______________

c. The biggest dilemma was solved by many kids. ______________

d. Bright students and good readers will enjoy this book. ______________

e. Those of you who like it might write another review. ______________

Spelling

Look, cover, write, check each word.

written ____________ ☐

suspense ____________ ☐

annually ____________ ☐

concentrate ____________ ☐

imagine ____________ ☐

particular ____________ ☐

character ____________ ☐

opportunity ____________ ☐

separate ____________ ☐

chronicle ____________ ☐

Word Building

Long vowel sound '**I**' as in '**eye**'
Say each word, **listen** to the **long** '**I**' **sound**

high	tide	bite	sigh
might	fight	light	bright
kite	skite	right	fright
alight	delight	quite	requite
mite	sight	night	invite
knight	digest	dilute	fire
file	hire	hide	higher

See how many you can write.

____

____

Sentences

Write whether each sentence is a **statement**, **question or command**.

a. *Secrets and Spies* is a non-fiction thriller. ____________

b. Do you agree? ____________

c. The text will be easy to read. ____________

d. In my view, this book will be good for anyone to read. ____________

e. So, get cracking for a good read! ____________

Chance

1. A box has 10 coloured balls in it; 5 red, 2 blue, 2 yellow and 1 green. Identify the chances of drawing coloured balls using these descriptors:

likely 50/50 unlikely impossible

a. A yellow ball ____________

b. A green ball ____________

c. A red ball ____________

d. A black ball ____________

2. Using the following descriptors of chance, complete these chance happenings.

unlikely 50/50 certain impossible

a. It will rain tomorrow ____________

b. I will toss a head with a coin ____________

Angles

1. Label each angle as **acute**, **obtuse**, **reflex**, **right** or **straight**.

a.

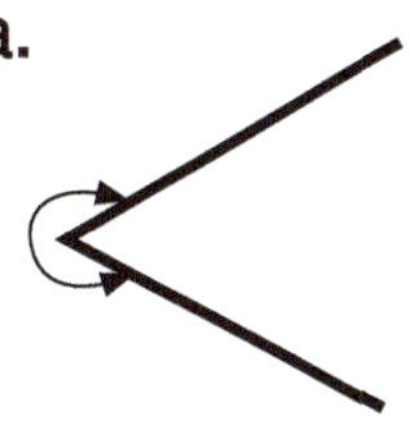

____

b.

____

c.

____

d.

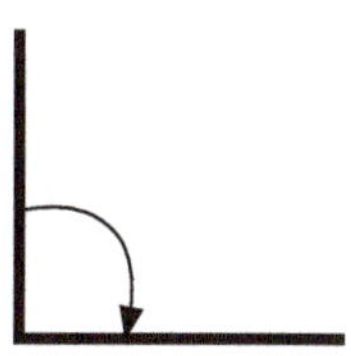

____

e.

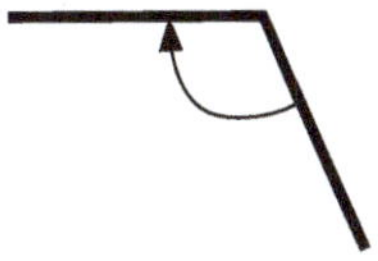

____

f.

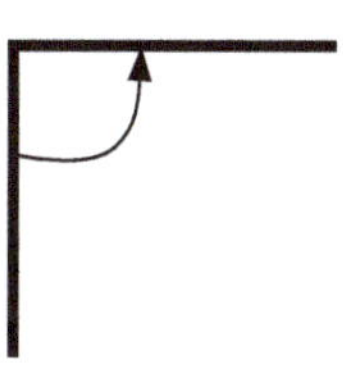

____

Glossary

Some Text Type Meanings

Text Type	*Meaning*
Argument	Putting forward a point of view
Description	Describing particular things about places, people or things
Exposition	Persuading either for or against a point of view
Explanation	Making it clear how to do things
Fable	A short tale that teaches a moral
Information	Providing specific and factual details
Narrative	A series of events with an unexpected outcome
Procedure	Outlining a way of doing a particular thing
Recount	Re-telling or recalling an event or story
Review	Writing about the content then describe and evaluate it

Understanding

Shade the bubble for the best answer.

a. Another name for a narrative is
- ◯ a recount
- ◯ a story
- ◯ a fable
- ◯ a poem

b. You will be able to put your point of view
- ◯ in a story
- ◯ in an explanation
- ◯ in a description
- ◯ in an exposition

c. To cook well you follow
- ◯ a recipe
- ◯ information
- ◯ procedure
- ◯ a description

d. Order 1 - 4 these words alphabetically
- ◯ procedure
- ◯ explanation
- ◯ exposition
- ◯ poem

Interpreting

Circle **T** (true) or **F** (false) to answer correctly.

a.	A persuasive text is another name for an exposition.	**T**	**F**
b.	Many narratives begin with "Once upon a time..."	**T**	**F**
c.	Good cooks often follow a procedure.	**T**	**F**
d.	Action verbs are used in a procedure.	**T**	**F**
e.	Adjectives are a strong feature in writing descriptions.	**T**	**F**

Language

Use **conjunctions** to compare and contrast in these sentences.

WORD BANK: as though like than therefore however

a. They all looked better__________________they did before.

b. We will go to town for lunch __________________ it could rain before then.

c. They were in such a rush, it was__________________ they couldn't wait.

d. Everyone looked __________________they needed to rest before dinner.

e. We all had the same amount, __________________ no one complained.

Spelling

Look, cover, write, check each word.

glossary ______________ ☐

argue ______________ ☐

describe ______________ ☐

persuade ______________ ☐

explain ______________ ☐

inform ______________ ☐

narrate ______________ ☐

proceed ______________ ☐

expose ______________ ☐

discuss ______________ ☐

Word Building

Nominalisation - nouns from verbs
Write each verb as a noun

a. argue ______________

b. describe ______________

c. persuade ______________

d. explain ______________

e. inform ______________

f. narrate ______________

g. proceed ______________

h. expose ______________

i. discuss ______________

Sentences

Write which text type fits each sentence best.

a. Once upon a time there were three bears... ______________

b. I think you should always do your best work. ______________

c. The blue house, belonging to my aunt, is for sale. ______________

d. The Sydney Harbour Bridge was opened in 1932. ______________

e. Take a piece of string, cut it into pieces and hang the ball. ______________

Capacity

1. Write the capacity showing on each cylinder.

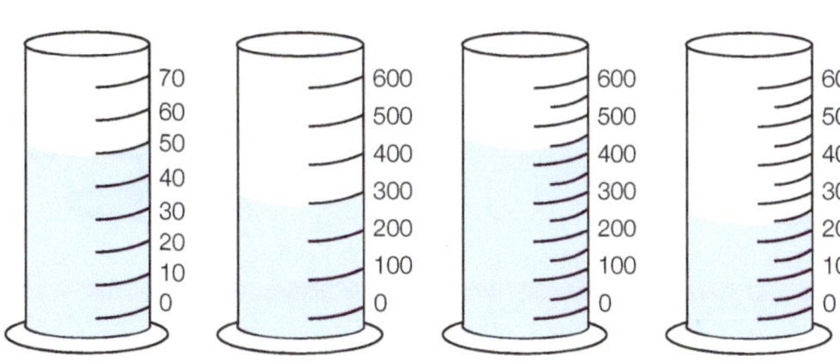

______ mL ______ mL ______ mL ______ mL

2. Shade the capacity that best matches each container.

a.

250L

25L

250mL

b.

250L

25L

250mL

Time

1. Write the time showing on each clock face in digital form.

a. **b.** **c.**

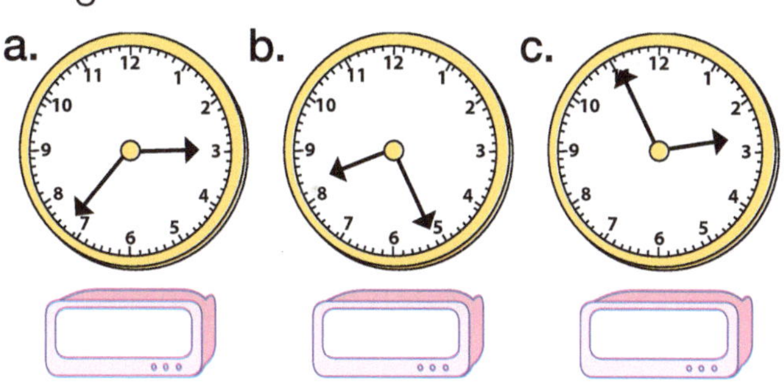

2. Write each time in its digital form.

a. Quarter to eleven ☐

b. Twenty-five to two ☐

3. If I catch a bus at 8:50 am and the trip takes 42 minutes, what time do I arrive at my destination. ______________

Should Parents Restrict Children's TV Viewing?

I believe that parents should restrict the TV viewing habits of their children.

I believe this because some of the shows that are on TV now days are not at all suitable for children. There is far too much violent content in many of the current shows. These shows are not meant to be viewed by children and are usually shown after 8:30 pm at night. But sometimes children are not in bed by then and they need their parents to stop them from viewing violent images.

It is often hard to police a type of violence being shown on the News bulletins though. There are some very sad images from war-torn places and especially where children are being killed. Parents can't stop children seeing these things because they don't know what will be shown and how gruesome it will be. When this happens parents should quickly turn to another channel or turn the TV off.

So, while it would be ideal if parents could select appropriate TV for their children to watch, sometimes this may not always be possible.

Understanding

Circle the best answer to each question

a. At what time does adult viewing being? 7.30 pm 8.30pm 9.30pm 10.30 pm

b. Should parents watch what children view? **Yes** **No**

c. Is violence often shown on news bulletins? **Yes** **No**

d. Do parents always know when violence will be shown? **Yes** **No**

e. It is always possible to stop children seeing violence on TV. **Yes** **No**

Interpreting

Tick the box if you can find this information in the text.

a. Children should not watch violent shows on TV. ☐
b. Many current shows on TV have violent content. ☐
c. News bulletins always have good news showing. ☐
d. You can see children in war-torn places on TV. ☐
e. Parents can turn the TV off when violence is showing. ☐

Language

Match these meanings:

a. violent content
b. hard to police
c. war-torn places
d. gruesome
e. images

f. pictures, videos
g. killing and destruction of life
h. horror, fear, terror
i. unable or difficult to control
j. Countries where fighting occurs

Spelling

Look, cover, write, check each word.

believe ______________ ☐
parents ______________ ☐
restrict ______________ ☐
suitable ______________ ☐
violent ______________ ☐
bulletin ______________ ☐
gruesome ______________ ☐
channel ______________ ☐
ideal ______________ ☐
especially ______________ ☐

Word Building

Silent 'e' at end of words.
Complete each word and say it aloud.

a. f_____me **b.** s _____ me
c. d_____me **d.** g _____ me
e. l _____ te **f.** m _____ te
g. r _____ ke **h.** f _____ ke
i. f _____ ce **j.** r _____ ce
k. pl _____ ce **l.** gr _____ ce
m. sh _____ ke **n.** sk _____ te
o. tr _____ ce **p.** cr _____ te
q. br _____ ce **r.** dr _____ ke
s. fr _____ me **t.** th _____ me

Sentences

Underline the most suitable modal adjective and/or adverb in each sentence.

a. The class will (probably, definitely) go on the excursion next week.
b. We (always, must, can) do an end of year concert for our parents.
c. Now we (might, perhaps, surely) have time to see the next picture.
d. I thought he (might, could) be relied upon to (definitely, may be) write.
e. Are you (sure, certain) they will (possibly, no doubt) be there to meet us.

Fractions

1. Colour the given fraction in each shape.

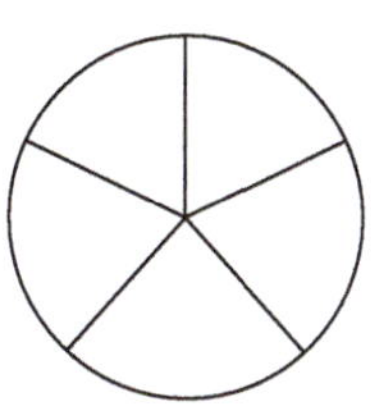

$\frac{4}{5}$

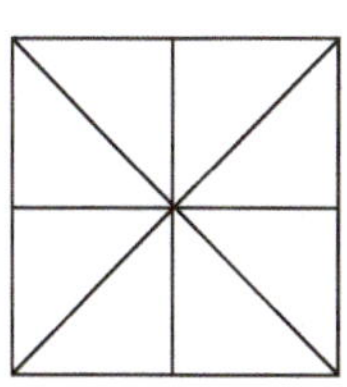

$\frac{5}{8}$

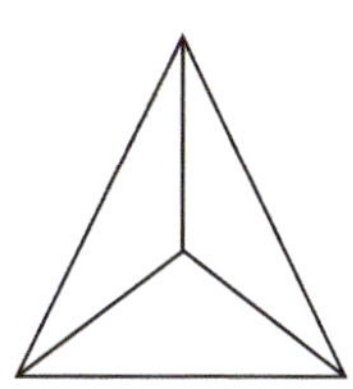

$\frac{2}{3}$

2. Write an equivalent fraction with a **lower denominator**.

a. $\frac{8}{10}$ = ___ **b.** $\frac{3}{6}$ = ___ **c.** $\frac{5}{10}$ = ___

d. $\frac{2}{4}$ = ___ **e.** $\frac{4}{10}$ = ___ **f.** $\frac{6}{8}$ = ___

g. How many halves in one? __________

h. A quarter of eight equals __________

X and ÷

1. Complete each number wheel.

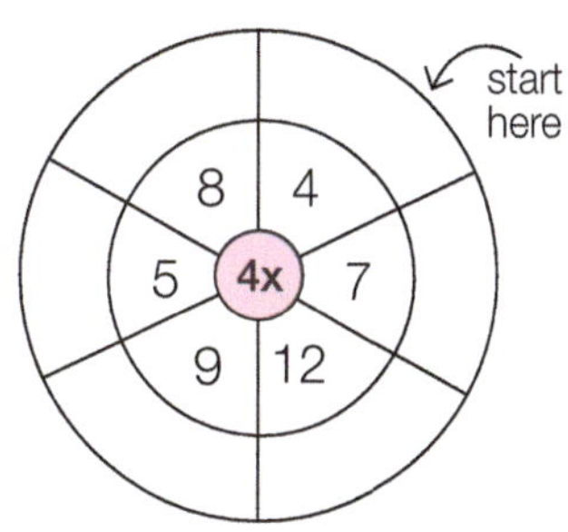

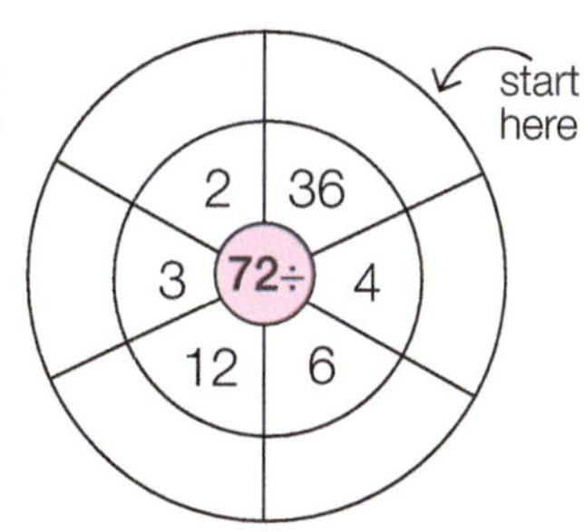

2. Complete these:

a. 60 divided by 5 = __________

b. 81 divided into 9 equal parts = __________

c. How many 4s in 28? = __________

d. 66 ÷ 11 = __________

Icarus

Here is another story from Greek mythology. It is the story of a boy called Icarus (Ic-a-rus) and his father Daedalus (Day-da-lus).

Daedalus and his son were prisoners of Minos, the King of Crete, in the Labyrinth invented by Daedalus. He did not like being kept prisoner so he had to think of a way to break out. The only way out was to fly!

So Daedalus began making two sets of wings so they could fly out. To do this he used wax to fix feathers onto a wooden frame. When the wings were finished, he gave one set to his son and told him not to fly too high to the sun because the sun's heat would melt the wax.

However, when Icarus put the wings on and began to fly he forgot his father's warning. When the wings started to come apart Icarus fell down into the sea and drowned. This made his father very sad.

Understanding

Fact or Opinion

Circle if the statement is a **fact** or an **opinion**

a. This would be a great way to fly. **Fact Opinion**

b. Icarus was Daedalus' son **Fact Opinion**

c. Icarus did not listen to his father's advice. **Fact Opinion**

d. I think this is a silly story. **Fact Opinion**

e. Early flight was a disaster. **Fact Opinion**

Interpreting

Circle **T** (true) or **F** (false) to answer correctly.

a. Daedalus was a prisoner. **T F**

b. Icarus was an old man. **T F**

c. The King of Crete was Minos. **T F**

d. Daedalus built the Labyrinth. **T F**

e. Daedalus wore the wings. **T F**

f. The wind did not blow. **T F**

g. The feathers melted. **T F**

h. The sun was too hot. **T F**

i. The wax melted. **T F**

j. Icarus flew too high. **T F**

Language

Write the **relating verb** in each sentence on the line.

a. A myth is a story that explains a natural happening. ____________________

b. Daedalus was a prisoner of Minos, the King of Crete. ____________________

c. Icarus and Daedalus were father and son. ____________________

d. They are two people very well known in Greek Mythology. ____________________

e. I am in the library looking for a book on Greek Mythology. ____________________

Unit 19

Spelling

Look, cover, write, check each word.

myth ______ ☐
mythology ______ ☐
prisoners ______ ☐
labyrinth ______ ☐
invented ______ ☐
feathers ______ ☐
wooden ______ ☐
finished ______ ☐
warning ______ ☐
drowning ______ ☐

Word Building

Drop the '**e**' and add '**ing**' to these words

a. love ______
b. note ______
c. come ______
d. shame ______
e. glue ______
f. taste ______
g. ache ______

Write the meaning of these two words

a. myth ______
b. labyrinth ______

Sentences

Write one word on the line for those in bold.

a. The **range of passages** was invented by Daedalus. ______

b. The **men in custody** were being transferred today. ______

c. We could consider our writing part of **an invented story.** ______

d. The motor car **was made up** for people to use and enjoy. ______

e. The **bird's quills** are used in products to keep people warm. ______

Decimal Fractions

1. Write each decimal as a hundredths fraction.

a. 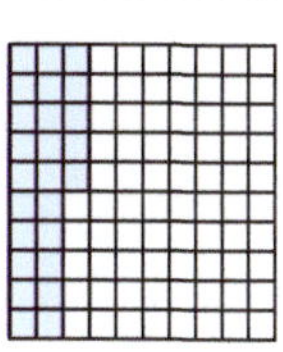 $\frac{\quad}{100}$

b. 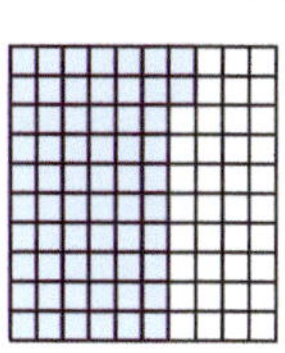 $\frac{\quad}{100}$

c. 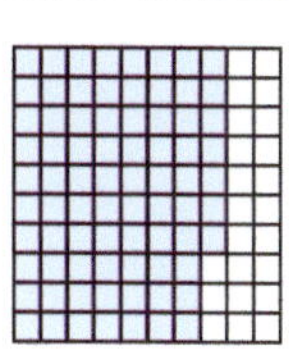 $\frac{\quad}{100}$

2. Write each fraction as a decimal.

a. $\frac{3}{4} = 0{\cdot}$______ **b.** $\frac{7}{10} = 0{\cdot}$______

c. $\frac{1}{2} = 0{\cdot}$______ **d.** $\frac{4}{5} = 0{\cdot}$______

e. $\frac{85}{100} = 0{\cdot}$______ **f.** $\frac{72}{100} = 0{\cdot}$______

3. Add the missing decimal.

0·3, 0·35, 0·4, 0·45, ☐, 0·55

Place Value

1. Write the number ten before each of these.

a. 61702 ______ **b.** 3812 ______

c. 7207 ______ **d.** 62798 ______

2. Write the place value for each circled number.

a. 83849 (circled: 8) ______

b. 72586 (circled: 8) ______

c. 37954 (circled: 3) ______

3. Arrange each group of numerals to make the **smallest** number.

a. 57263 ______ **b.** 87519 ______

c. 62738 ______ **d.** 75026 ______

Grandpa's Shed

This is the most amazing place on Earth! It has so much to delight everyone who walks into it. Just imagine all the possible sights - tools, equipment, ride-on mowers, tractors, sheet metal lathes, wood splitters and so many racks of timber with nails, screws and washers all set up along the wall in see-through containers.

Wow!! There is no floor space to speak of. It is full of all good things that have been collected over the years and are sure to come in handy, one day! These include a large table with a vice at one end. Fans and drums with metal stakes which can be used in the garden. There are empty flower pots to be reused for new pieces of shrub, which will be struck from others in grandma's garden. On the back wall there are many used and unused cans of paint. Oh, there are paint rollers and brushes as well!

Two bikes are there for my sister and me and a smaller one for our little niece. These were new a few years back and they are still in good condition today. If you look hard enough you will find some other toys that have been discarded but kept for someone else to use. Then there are the two 'fridges full of cans of soft drink for hot days and everyone to enjoy. Oh, what a collection!

Understanding

Circle **Yes** or **No** to answer each statement

a.	There are two bikes in grandpa's shed.	**Yes**	**No**
b.	You can find almost anything in this shed.	**Yes**	**No**
c.	There is plenty of floor space in this shed.	**Yes**	**No**
d.	Would the toys be still useful?	**Yes**	**No**
e.	Is there much in this shed to suit everyone?	**Yes**	**No**

Interpreting

Write an answer to each question

a. Is grandpa's shed in the city or the country? Explain your answer.

____

b. What are the metal stakes to be used for?

____

c. How many refrigerators are in the shed?

____

d. What will you find in the shed to drink?

____

e. How have things been collected for the shed? Why?

____

Language

Underline the best **comparative or superlative adjective** in each sentence.

a. Grandpa's shed is the (big, bigger, biggest) in the street.

b. This shed has the (longer, longest) rope of any I've seen.

c. These tins of paint are the (lighter, lightest) I could find.

d. The shed is the (good, best) around but dad's is (best, better).

e. The steak was (bad, worse), the chicken (bad, worse) but the fish was the (worse, worst).

Spelling

Look, cover, write, check each word.

- amazing ______ ☐
- equipment ______ ☐
- delight ______ ☐
- lathes ______ ☐
- condition ______ ☐
- containers ______ ☐
- collection ______ ☐
- possible ______ ☐
- discarded ______ ☐
- repairing ______ ☐

Word Building

Add the **Prefix** 'be' to these words

a. cause ______

b. come ______

c. came ______

d. fore ______

e. little ______

g. ware ______

Write in syllables -

h. condition ______

i. collection ______

Sentences

Use these words correctly in a sentence.

WORD BANK: tractor lathe collection amazing wood splitter

a. We all think Grandpa's Shed is ______ .

b. A ______ can be used to shape wood and metal.

c. We all love to ride on the ______ at the farm.

d. The ______ cuts large tree branches into firewood.

e. What a wonderful ______ of 'junk' Grandpa has!

Mixed Additions

1. Add these sums of money.

a.
$123.40
16.25
+162.38
$______

b.
$413.22
142.18
+234.15
$______

c.
$62.85
135.42
+201.66
$______

2. Add each number to the centre one.

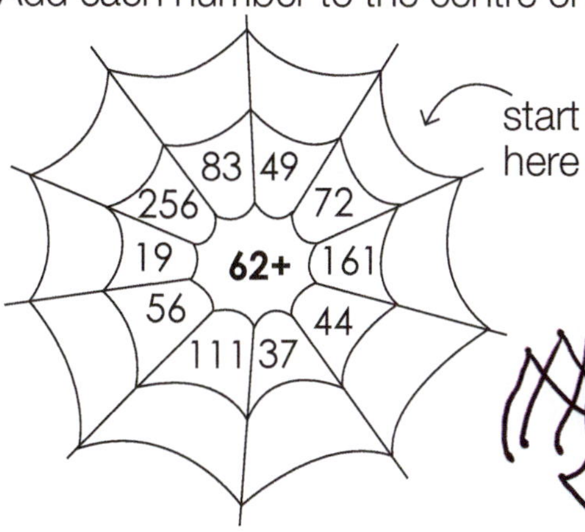

Mixed Bag

1. Complete each of these:

a. Double $\frac{1}{2}$ ______

b. $1\frac{1}{2}$ hours after 3:20 = ______

c. 1 375 cents = $ ______

d. Write $\frac{4}{5}$ as a decimal = ______

2. If there are 7 sets of twins at a school, 3 sets of triplets and one set of quadruplets, how many children at the school? ______

3. Use a calculator to help find your answer here.

a. 150 x 3 = ______ **b.** 2173 + 687 = ______

c. 900 ÷ 3 = ______ **d.** 0.16 + 0.76 = ______

An Acrostic Poem

Every building shakes
Another disaster awaits.
Right now we have to go
There is no time to waste!
How we will survive this time?
Quakes are so destructive
Until they happen there is no
Answer.
Killers they can come
Every time they
Strike

Use this sample to write your own poem

E ____________________
A ____________________
R ____________________
T ____________________
H ____________________
Q ____________________
U ____________________
A ____________________
K ____________________
E ____________________
S ____________________

Understanding

Circle **T** (true) or **F** (false) to answer correctly.

a. An earthquake is a disaster **T** **F**
b. Earthquakes are deadly **T** **F**
c. Earthquakes are natural disasters **T** **F**
d. Earthquakes happen overseas only **T** **F**
e. Earthquakes cause tsunamis **T** **F**

Interpreting

Shade the bubble for the best answer.

a. There was a deadly earthquake in
- ◯ Perth
- ◯ Brisbane
- ◯ Newcastle
- ◯ Melbourne

b. Which of these is a natural disaster?
- ◯ a drought
- ◯ a plane crash
- ◯ a train derailment
- ◯ an artificial event

c. Which word means 'famine'?
- ◯ food ◯ hunger
- ◯ plenty ◯ familiar

d. An epidemic is
- ◯ outbreak ◯ episode
- ◯ part ◯ period

Language

Underline the **helping verbs** and the **present participle** in each sentence.

a. I (done, am doing) my homework.

b. The boys and girls (sung, are singing) at the local shopping centre.

c. Many people (run, are running) in the Cancer Council Fun Run today.

d. The bell (rung, is ringing) for us to go into class.

Spelling

Look, cover, write, check each word.

- building ______________________ ☐
- disaster ______________________ ☐
- quell ______________________ ☐
- survive ______________________ ☐
- destroy ______________________ ☐
- destructive ______________________ ☐
- rumble ______________________ ☐
- energy ______________________ ☐
- quiver ______________________ ☐
- anxious ______________________ ☐

Word Building

Homophones - there, their, they're
Use each one correctly in the sentence

a. This is ____________ book.

b. When ____________ here, let me know.

c. Take ____________ money please.

d. Put it ____________ .

e. It is over ____________ .

f. ____________ going home now.

"**Q**" is followed by '**u**' except in QANTAS which is an acronym. Write more '**qu**'words

____

____

Sentences

Write the **verbs** (thoughts, feelings and opinions) in each sentence on the line.

a. Mia and Paris wished for a dry day for the wedding. ____________

b. It is thought to have been raining, but now they believe it will be dry. ____________

c. Do you remember when the last bus leaves? ____________

d. I wonder if it will hurt much because I feel sorry for him. ____________

e. Do consider what has to be done before you upset them. ____________

Locations

1. Follow the directions and draw each shape on the grid. The first one is done.

a. ☆ Up 1, 2 left	**f.** ✔ Down 1, 5 right
b. ◆ Up 3, 4 right	**g.** ✤ Up 4, 1 left
c. ➜ Down 1, 2 left	**h.** ✖ Down 1, 3 left
d. ♥ Up 2, 4 left	**i.** ■ Down 2, 3 left
e. ● Down 3, 2 left	

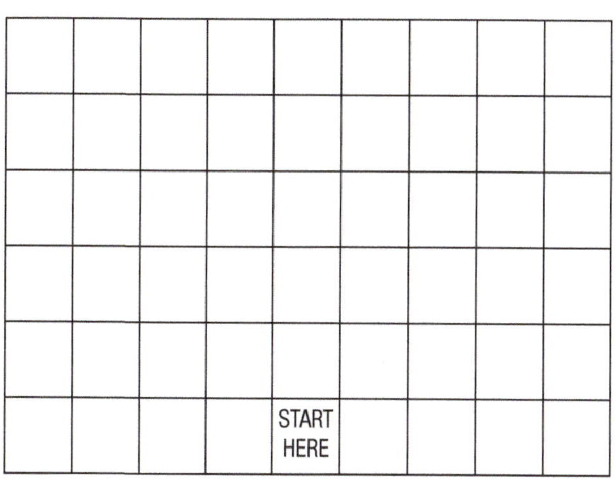

2. Write the co-ordinates for each shape.

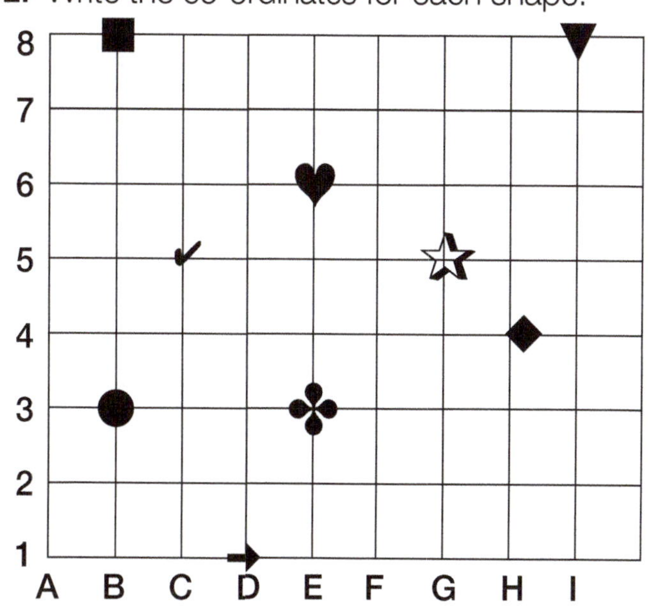

a. ☆ ________	**b.** ◆ ________	**c.** ■ ________
d. ● ________	**e.** ♥ ________	**f.** ▼ ________
g. ✤ ________	**h.** ✔ ________	**i.** ➜ ________

Making Paper Flowers

You will need -

Tissue paper OR Pretty Wrapping paper
Scissors
Coloured pipe cleaners – cut in half
Ribbon – cut into 12cm lengths
Dry tree branches

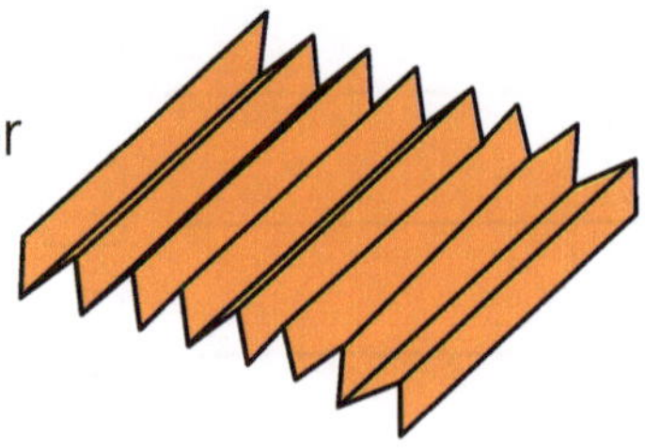

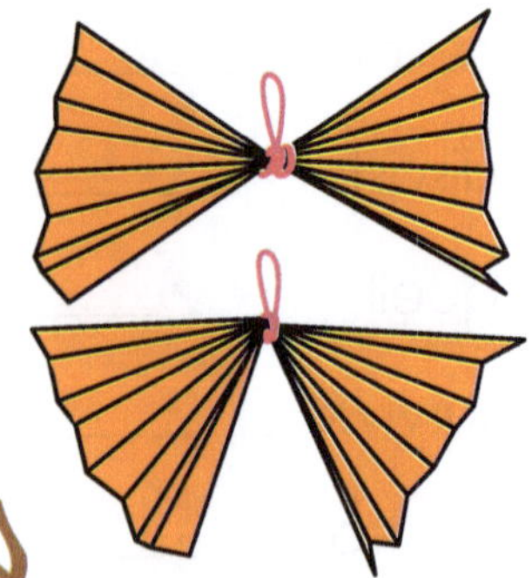

How to make the flower -

1. Place a few sheets of paper on top of one another
2. Carefully mark out rectangles 24cm by 16cm
3. Fold each set into 1 cm fan-like pieces
4. Twist a piece of pipe cleaner around the middle of the paper
5. Trim the ends of the paper to a rounded shape
6. Slip a piece of ribbon under the pipe cleaner
7. Hold the paper in the middle to separate each layer
8. Hang on the dry tree branches

Understanding

Order these steps from the instructions correctly.

a. Trim the ends ☐
b. Mark out rectangles ☐
c. Hang on dry tree branches ☐
d. Place paper on top of each other ☐
e. Slip ribbon under pipe cleaner ☐
f. Fold into 1cm fan-like pieces ☐

Interpreting

Circle **Yes** or **No** to answer each statement.

a. Would these flowers be easy to make?	**Yes**	**No**
b. Do you need help to make the flowers?	**Yes**	**No**
c. Are pipe cleaners easy to cut?	**Yes**	**No**
d. Can these flowers be made with any paper?	**Yes**	**No**
e. Will tissue paper flowers be more realistic?	**Yes**	**No**

Language

Match the **collective nouns** to the correct **noun group**.

bees players cards grapes sheep bananas ants cattle kittens children

a. a deck of ____________________
b. a hand of ____________________
c. a flock of ____________________
d. a swarm of ____________________
e. a herd of ____________________
f. a class of ____________________
g. a nest of ____________________
h. a litter of ____________________
i. a bunch of ____________________
j. a team of ____________________

Spelling

Look, cover, write, check each word.

- wrap ______________ ☐
- scissors ______________ ☐
- length ______________ ☐
- ribbon ______________ ☐
- branch ______________ ☐
- careful ______________ ☐
- middle ______________ ☐
- rounded ______________ ☐
- flowers ______________ ☐
- flour ______________ ☐

Word Building

Abbreviations with Capital Letters
Match each one to its meaning

a. RAAF	**h.** New Zealand
b. MP	**i.** United Nations
c. BA	**j.** European Union
d. UN	**k.** Royal Australian Air Force
e. NZ	**l.** Member of Parliament
f. SBS	**m.** Bachelor of Arts
g. EU	**n.** Special Broadcasting Service

Write the **homophones** in the list

____

Sentences

Write a **contraction** on the line for each word in bold.

a. The boys **did not** like to play cricket in that team. ______________

b. After a time they **were not** interested in the game. ______________

c. It was no wonder he **could not** go with his friends. ______________

d. I **shall not** be home when you call but **they will** be here. ______________

e. It **will not** be allowed if the principal hears about it. ______________

Capacity

1. Write the water level showing on each container.

a. 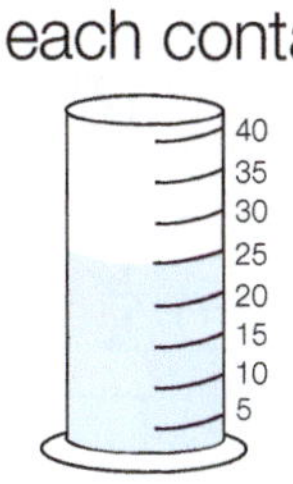

________ mL

b. 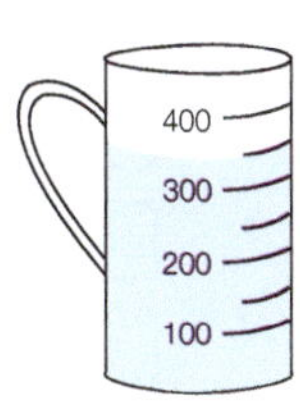

________ mL

c. 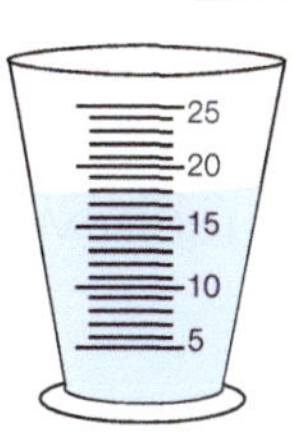

________ mL

d. 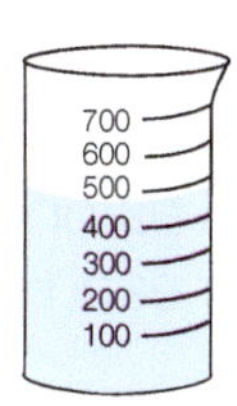

________ mL

2. How many millilitres in each of these?

a. 8Litres = ________ **b.** 2½ Litres = ________

c. ½ Litre = ________ **d.** ¾ Litre= ________

Money

1. Calculate the change after rounding off to the nearest five cents.

a. 

change from $50

____

b. 

change from $110

____

c. 

change from $50

____

d. 

change from $20

____

2. Dad bought a chocolate for $3.76. If he paid with a $5 note, what change would he receive? ________

Holidays should be Longer

It is my honest opinion that holidays should not be longer and I'll tell you why.

These days there is too much time spent just doing nothing. I don't like sitting around wanting to do things and not being able to do them. Because I live so far out of town, there is really nothing for me to do if I have too many holidays. Holidays are meant to be enjoyed but when there is nowhere to go and no one to have fun with then they can be boring.

When I go to school I can be with my great friends and have fun with them. I have to travel a long way on the bus to school but I don't mind that. I get up early to catch it and then I have a lot of time to be with my mates because they get on the bus too. When we get to school we play games and just enjoy being with each other. Then we go into school. It's good to be with friends at school.

So in my opinion I don't believe that holidays should be longer. If there is nothing to do and nowhere to go then holidays are boring and a waste of time!

Understanding

Circle **F** (fact) or **O** (Opinion) for each statement

a. The writer doesn't believe holidays should be longer? F O
b. We have far too many holidays. F O
c. Parents don't like too many holidays. F O
d. You just do nothing when there are too many holidays. F O
e. Holidays are for people to relax and enjoy themselves. F O
f. Friends can be great fun to be with sometimes. F O
g. Holidays are boring if there is nowhere to go. F O

Interpreting

Tick the box if the information is in the text.

a. There is no reason to have longer holidays. ☐
b. It is boring to have too many holidays. ☐
c. Living out of town has its drawbacks. ☐
d. It is good to play games with friends before school. ☐
e. Holidays can be a waste of time for some people. ☐
f. Everyone should get up early to go to school. ☐

Language

Use a **singular verb** with a **collective noun** referring to a group as one unit. Eg. The team was …
Underline the collective noun and cross out the incorrect verb in each sentence.

a. "No one (are, is) away sick this week," said the teacher.
b. The gang of thieves (were, was) frightening the shopkeepers.
c. There (are, is) a litter of pups for sale in the Pet shop today.
d. The choir (are, is) singing Christmas Carols at this year's concert.
e. The neighbour (are, is) complaining because the herd (are, is) on the road.

Spelling

Look, cover, write, check each word.

honest ______________ ☐

wanting ______________ ☐

holiday ______________ ☐

boring ______________ ☐

friends ______________ ☐

travel ______________ ☐

should ______________ ☐

nothing ______________ ☐

nowhere ______________ ☐

waste ______________ ☐

Word Building

Words beginning with silent '**g**'
Match the word to its meaning.

a. gnome
b. gnat
c. gnash
d. gnarled
e. gnaw

f. grind (the teeth)
g. wrinkled
h. to bite
i. a small bat
j. little, old man

Add the **prefix** '**be**' to make new words

a. come ______________

b. ware ______________

c. cause ______________

Sentences

Use the present participle with ***past tense verbs - were or was.***

WORD BANK: were reading was swimming were running were looking was getting

a. Before long, we ______________ for our lives.

b. It ______________ dark and we had to rush home.

c. When our dog was lost we ______________ for it everywhere.

d. Can you let me know who ______________ in that race.

e. The teachers ______________ the names of the competitors.

Shapes and Angles

1. Colour each shape in the tangram and then name each shape.

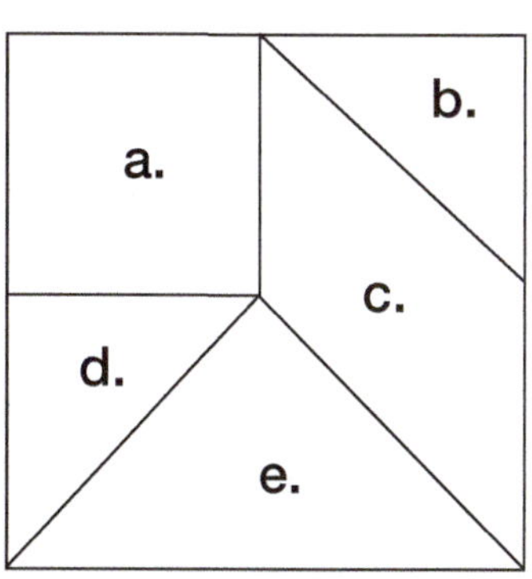

a. ______________
b. ______________
c. ______________
d. ______________
e. ______________

2. Record the angle types in the tangram.

a. There are ☐ right angles.

b. There are ☐ obtuse angles.

c. There are ☐ acute angles.

Perimeter

1. Measure the perimeter of this shape.

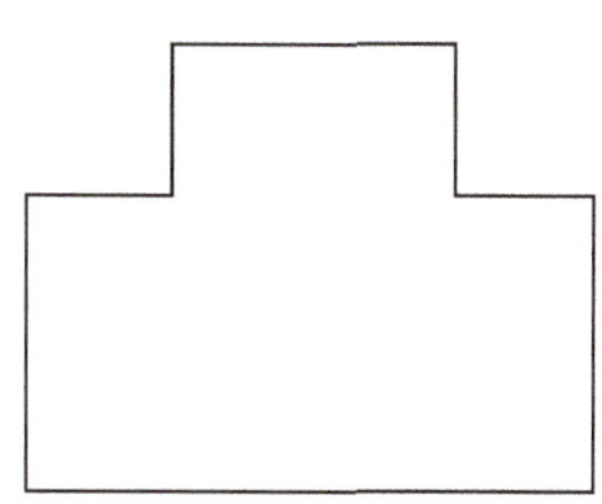

Perimeter = ☐ cm

2. Find the perimeter of this shape.

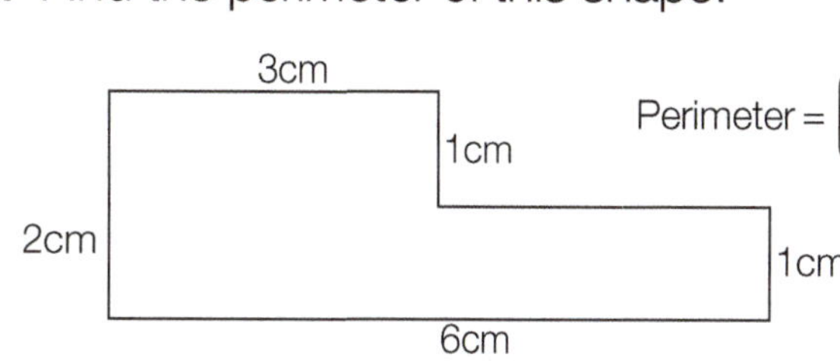

Perimeter = ☐ cm

An Invitation by Electronic Mail

To:	billg09@gmail.com
From.	samt08@gmail.com
Subject:	Birthday Party

Dear Bill

This Saturday I am having a party at my house beginning at 2 pm and I would like you to come. We should have a good time because mum has been busy making lots of goodies for us to eat. We are going to play some new games we bought this week and some old ones we got for Christmas too. I have invited all our friends and some of my relatives. Don't worry if you think you don't know them, they are great kids and mix in easy with everyone. Mum says the party should be over by 5 pm so could you let your mum know to pick you up about then please?

Please reply as soon as possible, or asap, if you can come.

Your buddy
Sam

Understanding

Circle **T** (True) of **F** (False) to answer correctly.

a. Bill is having a birthday party. **T** **F**

b. It will early in the day. **T** **F**

c. Relatives will be at the party. **T** **F**

d. Dad will cook for us. **T** **F**

e. Sam has sent this invitation. **T** **F**

f. Dad will take you home **T** **F**

g. There will be games to play. **T** **F**

h. The party is after Christmas **T** **F**

Interpreting

Write an answer to each question.

a. How many people will be at the party? ______________________

b. How can Bill respond to Sam? ______________________

c. What is Sam's Email address? ______________________

d. What is the domain name for Bill? ______________________

e. What do the letters 'asap' mean? ______________________

Language

Use **have, or has** with some past tense verbs.

has rung   have seen   have done   has seen

a. I **did** my homework. **BUT** **a.** I **have done** my homework.

b. She **rang** the bell. **BUT** **b.** She ______________ the bell.

c. They **saw** the clowns. **BUT** **c.** They ______________ the clowns.

d. We **did** the cleaning. **BUT** **d.** We ______________ the cleaning.

e. She **saw** the koala. **BUT** **e.** She ______________ the koala.

Spelling

Look, cover, write, check each word.

Saturday ______ ☐

Wednesday ______ ☐

beginning ______ ☐

relatives ______ ☐

birthday ______ ☐

bought ______ ☐

buy ______ ☐

bring ______ ☐

brought ______ ☐

invitation ______ ☐

Word Building

More silent letters to begin words - **‘k’** & **‘h’**
Write the meaning of-

a. knot ______

b. know ______

c. knife ______

d. knead ______

e. knight ______

f. knave ______

g. honour ______

h. honest ______

i. honorary ______

j. honorific ______

Sentences

Use each word correctly in a sentence

WORD BANK: bought buy bring brought

a. I went to town to ______ a present for Sam’s birthday

b. I did not have to ______ anything with me to the party.

c. When I ______ the present, I went straight home to mum.

d. Everyone ______ great presents to Sam’s birthday party.

e. ______ the books to school that you ______ for me.

Fractions

1. Write the fraction for the shaded part.

a.

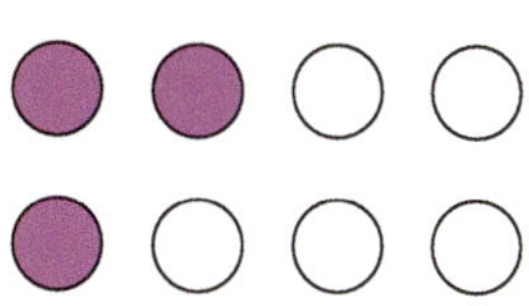

$\frac{\square}{\square}$

b.

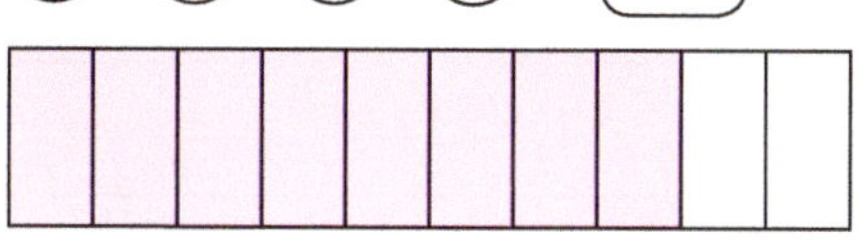

$\frac{\square}{\square}$

c.

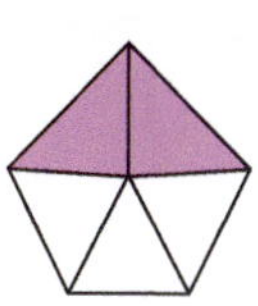

$\frac{\square}{\square}$

d.

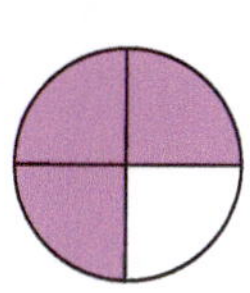

$\frac{\square}{\square}$

2. What fraction is 17 out of 100? $\frac{\square}{\square}$

3. $\frac{64}{100}$ as a decimal. ______

Division

1. Complete these simple divisions.

a. 56 ÷ 7 = ☐ **b.** 48 ÷ 6 = ☐

c. 64 ÷ 8 = ☐ **d.** 81 ÷ 9 = ☐

e. ☐ ÷ 4 = 9 **f.** ☐ ÷ 6 = 7

g. 72 ÷ ☐ = 8 **h.** 45 ÷ ☐ = 5

2. Try each division in the contracted form.

a. $3\overline{)18}$ **b.** $4\overline{)32}$ **c.** $6\overline{)54}$

d. $2\overline{)48}$ **e.** $3\overline{)39}$ **f.** $4\overline{)84}$

Our Christmas Toy Sale

Understanding Shade the bubble for the best answer.

a. When can you get these toys?
- ◯ During the year
- ◯ While stocks last
- ◯ Only at Christmas
- ◯ Whenever there is time

b. Where would you find this type of sale?
- ◯ at the supermarkets
- ◯ at the bicycle sales
- ◯ at very big toy shops
- ◯ at any recycled toy sale

c. How many toys are offered for sale?
- ◯ not many
- ◯ about fifty
- ◯ about one hundred
- ◯ more than one hundred

d. When should you get these toys?
- ◯ before Christmas
- ◯ as soon as possible
- ◯ whenever you can
- ◯ when you go shopping

Interpreting Write an answer to each question.

a. Why do people lay-by toys for Christmas? ____________________

b. What is a catalogue? ____________________

c. Why does it say 'stocks won't last'? ____________________

d. Why do you think the toys are reduced for the sale? ____________________

e. How can you buy toys at this sale? ____________________

Language Write the **verb** in bold in the **future tense** on the line. **Hint:** Use will … to show future tense.

a. We **are having** a party today. ____________________

b. He **is going** to work on the bus. ____________________

c. Dad **is finished** work now. ____________________

d. Who **is playing** football for us? ____________________

Spelling

Unit 25

Look, cover, write, check each word.

reduced ______ ☐

early ______ ☐

hundreds ______ ☐

specials ______ ☐

catalogue ______ ☐

season ______ ☐

on-line ______ ☐

quick ______ ☐

treat ______ ☐

Christmas ______ ☐

Word Building

Build words using '**every**' with each word
Write the new word

a. body ______

b. where ______

c. thing ______

d. one ______

e. day ______

Write each word in the **past tense**

a. bring ______

b. buy ______

c. run ______

d. see ______

Sentences

Use these verbs correctly in a sentence.

WORD BANK: ran saw bought brought

a. We went to the shops and ______ all our Christmas presents.

b. Everyone ______ after the ice-cream van.

c. We were so amazed when we ______ what had happened.

d. The girls ______ everything we needed for the picnic.

Decimals

1. Arrange these in **descending** order.

$\frac{4}{10}$, $\frac{7}{10}$, $\frac{4}{5}$, 0.3, $\frac{1}{2}$, $\frac{1}{10}$

______

2. Add these decimals.

a. 1.2 + 2.7 = ____

b. 5.3 + 2.4 = ____

c. 16.3 + 12.6 = ____

d. 7.3 + 2.2 = ____

3. Add these sums of money

a. \$24.32 + \$34.53 = ____

b. \$62.38 + \$12.41 = ____

c. \$52.63 + \$ 7.34 = ____

X and ÷ Equivalents

1. Complete these simple divisions.

a. 8 x ☐ = 48 ÷ ☐ = 8

b. 9 x ☐ = 63 ÷ ☐ = 9

2. Try these multiplications and divisions.

a. 25 x 4 = ____

b. 37 x 3 = ____

c. 62 x 6 = ____

d. 2)48

e. 3)39

f. 4)84

3. PROBLEMS

Twenty eight girls are divided into four groups. How many girls in each group? ______

Our End of Year Concert

Year 4 extends an invitation to ______________________________

To attend Our End of Year Concert

To be held in: *Our main school Assembly Hall*

Commencing at: *2:30 pm* On: *Wednesday, 1 December*

To enable us to plan our seating and catering arrangements it would be appreciated if you could notify your acceptance of this invitation by Monday, 29 November, to

The Year 4 Organising Committee

Understanding

Circle **Yes** or **No** to answer each statement.

a. The concert will start 2:30pm **Yes No**

b. Refreshments will be served. **Yes No**

c. The concert is on 29 November. **Yes No**

d. Everyone is invited to come. **Yes No**

e. A seat will be allocated to you. **Yes No**

f. Year 4 is performing. **Yes No**

g. Is this a regular concert? **Yes No**

h. Is it in the school hall? **Yes No**

Interpreting

Write an answer to each question.

a. What is the line for at the top of the invitation? ______________________

b. Who would you invite to this concert? ______________________

c. Why should you reply to an invitation? ______________________

d. Is it important to reply to this invitation? ______________________

e. Would *you* receive this invitation? Why? ______________________

Language

Use these **feeling verbs** to complete each sentence.

WORD BANK: hurt upset worry enjoy calm

a. Do not be too ______________________ if you can't attend the concert.

b. We hope everyone will ______________________ this concert.

c. We shall all remain ______________________ if we make any mistakes.

d. If we fall off the stage we could ______________________ ourselves.

e. Our teacher will ______________________ if our main characters get sick.

Unit 26

Spelling

Look, cover, write, check each word.

extends ______________ ☐

invitation ______________ ☐

attend ______________ ☐

concert ______________ ☐

assembly ______________ ☐

commence ______________ ☐

catering ______________ ☐

enable ______________ ☐

arrangements ______________ ☐

committee ______________ ☐

Word Building

Add '**ing**' to these words. Write the new word on the line. **NB**: Some drop the 'e'

a. extend ______________

b. attend ______________

c. invite ______________

d. hope ______________

e. enable ______________

f. arrange ______________

Write these words in syllables.

a. invitation ______________

b. arrangements ______________

c. committee ______________

Sentences

Abstract nouns and **feeling verbs** happen in your head. Eg. (to be) happy - happiness
Use these abstract nouns correctly in each sentence. **sadness, amusement, pleasure**

a. Animals give their owners great ______________ .

b. There was a great deal of ______________ at the concert.

c. Everyone felt much ______________ when the team lost the grand final.

Maps and Location

1. Study the map and its co-ordinates to complete the activities.

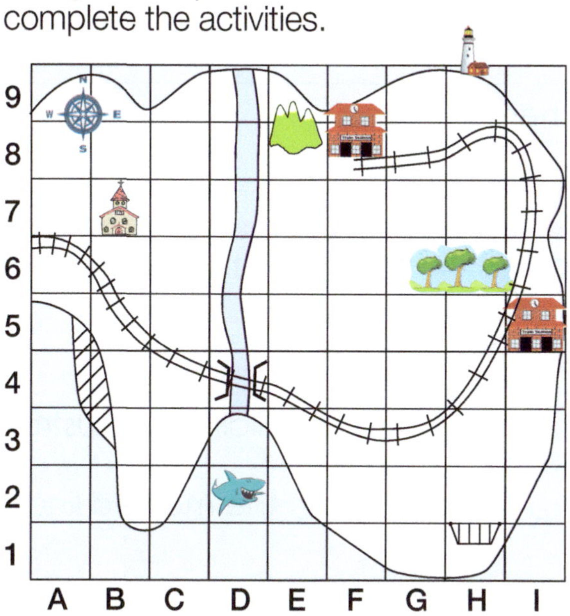

Key church, bridge, railway station, Shark Bay, railway, lighthouse, forest, mountains, beach, river, lookout

a. Write the co-ordinates for the lighthouse. ______________

b. What can be found at B7? ______________

c. Write the co-ordinates for the railway bridge over the river. ______________

d. Where is the lookout situated? ______________

e. Where does the railway finish? ______________

f. Write the co-ordinates for the forest area. ______________

g. What can be found at I4? ______________

h. How many beaches on the map? ______________

i. In which direction does the river flow? ______________

What Do You See?

Understanding Circle **T** (True) of **F** (False) to answer correctly.

a.	There are two animals on the Australian Coat of Arms.	**T**	**F**
b.	Parliament House is in Canberra.	**T**	**F**
c.	The National Capital is Canberra.	**T**	**F**
d.	The Southern Cross is on the Australian Flag.	**T**	**F**
e.	Both flags fly on the Sydney Harbour Bridge.	**T**	**F**

Interpreting Write the questions to which these are the answers.

a. There is a kangaroo and an emu on the Australian Coat of Arms.

____

b. It connects the southern side of Sydney to the north.

____

c. It has seven points representing the five states and two territories.

____

d. It is the biggest monolith in the World in the Northern Territory.

____

Language **Adverbs of place** add meaning to a verb. Use the following correctly in a sentence.

WORD BANK: nearby, above, close, beyond, between

a. Flags are flying ____________________ all government buildings in Australia.

b. There are many reasons not to go ____________________ the marked lines.

c. What is ____________________ Brisbane and Canberra?

d. Will you be ____________________ to Uluru on your trip north?

e. I know the pedestrian walkway is ____________________ .

Spelling

Look, cover, write, check each word.

parliament ______________ ☐

Australia ______________ ☐

Aboriginal ______________ ☐

Uluru ______________ ☐

Didgeridoo ______________ ☐

Canberra ______________ ☐

Aborigine ______________ ☐

indigenous ______________ ☐

territory ______________ ☐

national ______________ ☐

Word Building

Homophones - to, too, two
Use each one correctly in the sentence

a. Here are_____ books.

b. Go_____ the shop for me_____.

c. He put that_____ me.

d. These_____ people went_____ town.

e. The_____ cars went_____ fast.

f. It is_____ wet_____ play now.

g. There are_____ flags on the page.

h. We went_____ the shop_____ buy eggs.

i. I went_____ buy_____ eggs_____.

j. They bought_____ cakes_____ eat.

Sentences

Use each word correctly in a sentence.

WORD BANK: Uluru Aboriginal Parliament National Flag

a. The Australian ______________ is located in Canberra.

b. The ______________ Capital of Australia is Canberra..

c. The Australian ______________ is on the flagpole at Parliament House.

d. Many ______________ people live on native lands near ______________.

Shopping

1. Add the cost of these goods and then round off to the nearest 5 cents.

a.

☐ + ☐ + ☐ + ☐ = $ _______

2. Round the change from $20 for each item.

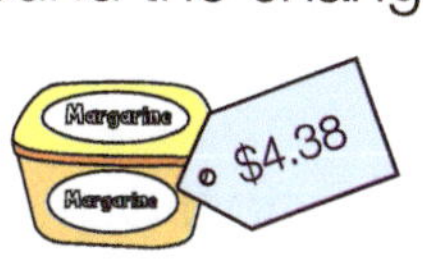

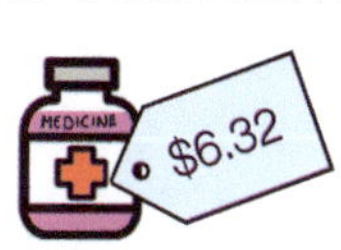

Change $_______ Change $_______

Money and Change

1. Round off each price to the nearest 5 cents. Give the change from $50.

a.

Change $_______

b.

Change $_______

c.

Change $_______

d.

Change $_______

2. What change would you get from $20 for the flower pot? _______

The Noisy Cicada

Cicadas live and grow for many years underground before they emerge in the open.

They begin life as a tiny black egg which the mother lays in the bark of a gum tree. When the eggs hatch the baby cicada falls to the ground and disappears overnight beneath the ground. It is here that they live their life as a nymph in tiny, dark spaces they have made for themselves. These spaces can often be 5-6 metres underground!

After many years, they begin to grow bigger, moult their skins and grow bigger again. Finally, they come up from their underground habitats. Now they are soft and pale with long, transparent wings but soon become dark in colour with strong wings. They are ready for life in the summer sunshine.

The noise made by a cicada happens when the muscles on its abdomen move in and out. Only the male cicada makes the loud noise that can be heard when summer days begin. Fossils have been found that prove these creatures have been around for over 400 years.

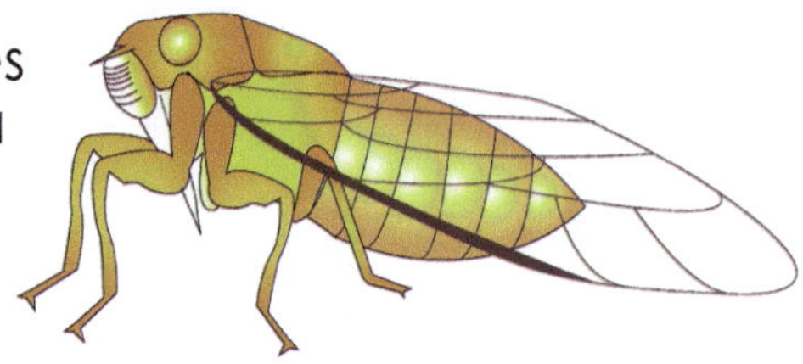

Understanding

Tick the box if the information is in the text.

a. Cicadas lay their eggs in the bark of gum trees. ☐

b. It takes a long time for a cicada to emerge. ☐

c. Cicadas live in tiny, dark spaces a long way underground. ☐

d. Before they emerge in the open the cicada moults and grows big. ☐

e. If you rub the abdomen of the cicada it will make a very loud noise. ☐

f. Only male cicadas make a noise. ☐

Interpreting

Where might you find this text? Tick as many as you wish.

a. In the library ☐	**b.** In a science book ☐
c. on a wall poster ☐	**d.** In a newspaper ☐
e. in a magazine ☐	**f.** on the Internet ☐
g. in an encyclopaedia ☐	**h.** in a book about insects ☐

Language

Use this technical language correctly.

moults, nymph, habitats, transparent, muscles, abdomen

a. The cicada is soft and pale with ______________________ wings.

b. When the cicada grows bigger it ______________________ its skin.

c. The ________________ on its ________________ move in and out.

d. You will find cicada ________________ very deep underground.

Spelling

Look, cover, write, check each word.

emerge ______ ☐
hatches ______ ☐
disappears ______ ☐
nymph ______ ☐
moult ______ ☐
habitat ______ ☐
transparent ______ ☐
muscles ______ ☐
abdomen ______ ☐
creatures ______ ☐

Word Building

Write the meaning of each of these words.

a. emerge ______
b. moult ______
c. habitat ______
d. abdomen ______
e. transparent ______
f. muscles ______

Write the list words with three syllables.

______
______
______

Sentences

Underline the **descriptive adjectives** in each sentence.

a. A cicada begins life as a tiny, black egg.
b. It grows for many years underground.
c. They live in tiny, dark places underground.
d. The habitat can be five to six metres deep.
e. They are soft and pale with long wings.
f. The transparent wings are see-through wings.
g. The loud noise is made only by the male.
h. On hot days and cool nights you hear them.

Time and Travel

1. Here are arrival and departure times for some planes at Sydney Airport.

DESTINATION	DEPARTURE	ARRIVAL
Melbourne	7:35 am	8:52 am
Adelaide	7:45 am	10:55 am
Brisbane	8:02 am	9:22 am
Perth	8:12 am	2:02 am
Canberra	8:15 am	9:05 am
Hobart	8:40 am	10:10 am
Darwin	8:50 am	12:48 am

a. What is the length of time taken to travel from Sydney on the 7:35 am plane to Melbourne? ______

b. What is the travel time from Sydney to Perth? ______

c. At what time does the plane leave Sydney for Adelaide? ______

d. How long is the Sydney to Adelaide journey? ______

e. How long is the Sydney to Canberra journey? ______

f. If I have to be in Brisbane by 9:30 am what time plane must I catch from Sydney? ______

2. Complete each time problem.

a. If the footy match starts at 1:35 pm and goes for 90 minutes, including stoppages, what time does the game finish? ______

b. How long from 4:20 pm 'till 6:55 pm? ______

Is Anybody There?

It was the beginning of the trip across the rocky shore and it had not started out well. First, they had underestimated the distance they needed to go and then there were the rocks! These rocks had long been the reason many people had not been able to finish their hike.

"Why can't you keep up?" cried Ali.
"Because it's too hard to crawl over these rocks and stay upright!" yelled Malia.

Often, when it was wet and cold, the rocks became slippery and too difficult to negotiate. They were now at the most dangerous part of their hike and the daylight was coming to a quick close. If they didn't get around the rocks soon they could be trapped there all night and they had no warm clothes or shelter. Being caught in extreme cold often causes death. The girls certainly didn't want that to happen.

That's when they saw a faint light in the distance. They cried out together.
"Is anybody there?" But there was no reply.
All they could do now was pick themselves up and hurry on before it was too late and too dark.

Understanding

Shade the bubble for the best answer.

a. What is the main problem in this story?
- ◯ the girls were lost
- ◯ the rocks were slippery
- ◯ there was no one there
- ◯ they could not be saved

b. 'underestimated' means
- ◯ restricted
- ◯ under valued
- ◯ wrong judgement
- ◯ below an estimation

c. Which statement is true?
- ◯ It was hot and dry
- ◯ the rocks were easy to climb
- ◯ they were trapped all night
- ◯ they saw a faint light in the distance

d. How was the story resolved?
- ◯ they climbed the rocks
- ◯ someone rescued them
- ◯ they hurried home before dark
- ◯ they cried out together

Spelling

Look, cover, write, check each word.

- begin ________ ☐
- distance ________ ☐
- crawl ________ ☐
- slippery ________ ☐
- difficult ________ ☐
- negotiate ________ ☐
- clothes ________ ☐
- extreme ________ ☐
- upright ________ ☐
- daylight ________ ☐

Word Building

Some words double the last consonant to add '**ing**'.

a. begin *beginning*
b. plan ________
c. clap ________
d. wrap ________
e. sun ________
f. prefer ________
g. regret ________
h. forget ________
i. omit ________
j. travel ________

1. Write if the word in bold is used as an **adjective or adverb** in each sentence.

a. The **anxious** parents were **here**. **anxious** ______ **here** ______

b. The **noisy** cicada sang **loudly**. **noisy** ______ **loudly** ______

c. **Many** people were **outside**. **Many** ______ **outside** ______

2. **Demonstrative Adjectives** can be singular (this or that) or plural (these or those)
Circle the correct adjective in each sentence.

a. Who owns (this, these) books?

b. To whom does (these, this) book belong?

c. On and off (these, that) light shines.

d. How far will (this, these) tapes reach?

3. **Change the gender** of the noun or pronoun in each sentence.

a. She is late for her appointment and her mother is late too.

______

b. My uncle is very ill and he will be in hospital until he is well.

______

c. There were twenty boys and five girls in the class and a male teacher.

______

4. **Punctuate** each sentence correctly.

a. the national capital of australia is canberra

______

b. we are going to the capitol to see the sound of music

______

c. lisa and irene were having lunch at the broadbeach hotel

______

Area

1. Which unit of area - m^2 or cm^2 - would you use for these?

a. 
1½ ______

b. 
2 ______

c. 
150 ______

d. 

625 ______

e. 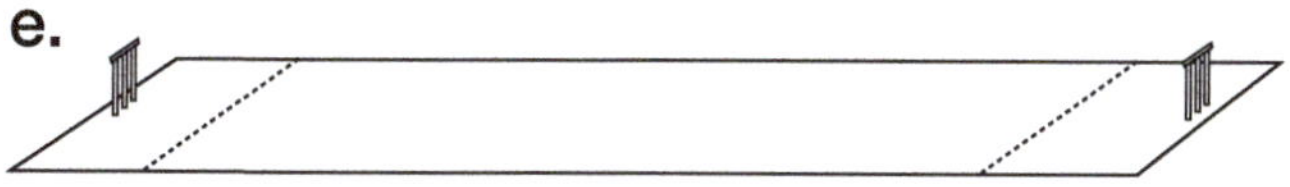
66 ______

Factors

1. Write the factors of each number.

a. 12 = ______

b. 20 = ______

c. 18 = ______

2. Write the missing factor in each number wheel.

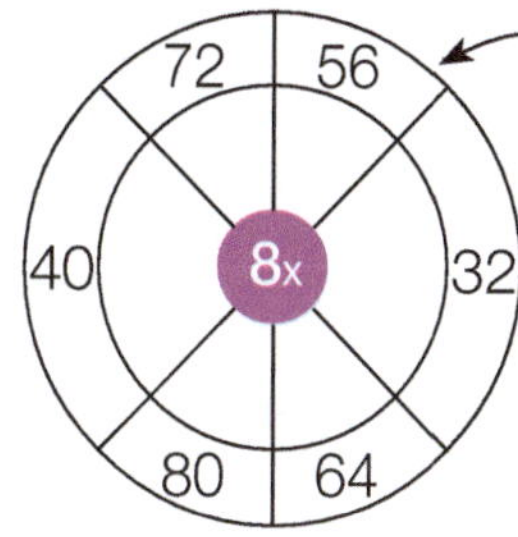

start here

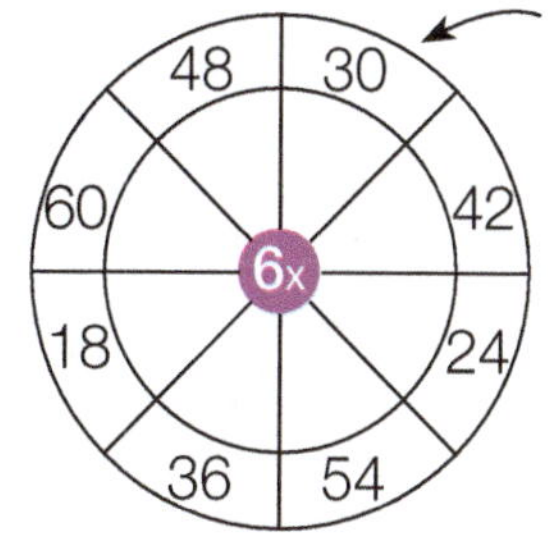

start here

Answers

Unit 1	**Understanding: a.** the howling wind **b.** the power lines had fallen **c.** calm everyone **d.** there were no batteries in the torch **e.** a cyclonic depression **/ Interpreting: a.** F **b.** F **c.** T **d.** T **e.** T **/ Language**: **a.** frightening **b.** howling **c.** exploding **d.** passing **e.** rising **f.** dark **g.** favourite swimming **/ Spelling:** Parent **/ Word Building:** parent check **/ Editing:** His book is overdue by now. **/ Sentences: a.** after dinner **b.** during the night **c.** In the morning **d.** before noon **/ Place Value: 1a.**4382 **b.**3567 **2 a.** 4 767 **b.** 8 245 **c.** 9 671 **/ Addition: 1a.** 35 **b.** 80 **c.** 47 **d.** 72 **e.** 93 **f.** 100 **2a.** 770 **b.** 589 **c.** 579 **d.** 4 597 **e.** 7 868
Unit 2	**Understanding:** tick **a. c. d. e. / Interpreting: a.** termite **b.** gooey **c.** suckle **d.** indigenous **e.** female **f.** hatch **g.** platypus **h.** mammal **/ Language: a.** huge **b.** large **c.** tiring **d.** scrumptious **e.** answered **f.** replied **/ Spelling:** Parent **/ Word Building: a.** gloves **b.** young **c.** protect **d.** tongue **e.** suckle **f.** native **g.** mammal **h.** people **/ Unjumbled:** monotreme **/ Sentences:** match **a - g**; **b - h**; **c - f**; **d - e / Odds and Evens: 1.** 9,7,15,31,13,19 **2.** 21, 23, 25, 27, 29 3. 42, 44, 46, 48 **/ Subtraction: 1a.** 21 **b.** 46 **c.** 58 **d.** 12 **e.** 12 **f.** 58 **2a.** 252 **b.** 722 **c.** 322
Unit 3	**Understanding:** Shade **a.** 3; **b.** 2; **c.** 4; **d.** 3 **/ Interpreting: a.** America **b.** Cosmonaut **c.** Valentina Tereshkova **d.** Russia **e.** It was the first to orbit the Earth and it carried a dog. **/ Language: a.** NASA **b.** ISS **/ Spelling:** Parent **/ Word Building:** match **a-k**; **b-j**; **c-g**; **d-h**; **e-l**; **f-l**; **/ Sentences: a.** Subject I, Verb am going **b.** Subject Astronauts, Verb are **c.** Subject Jon, Verb cried **d.** Subject Twenty people Verb saw **e.** Subject Our teacher Verb shouted **/ Angles: 1a.** obtuse **b.** reflex **c.** right **d.** acute **e.** straight **f.** obtuse **/ Time: 1a.** 9:27 am **b.** 7:35 am **c.** 10:54 am **2a.** 11:35 **b.** 9:30 **c.** 6:25 **3a.** 6:12 7:12 **b.** 6:59 7:59
Unit 4	**Understanding:** tick - **a,c,f,g,h,l,j / Interpreting: a.** To go under the railway line to the other side. **b.** No. There are not many streets on the map. **c.** Melbourne Street **d.** It is the last street in town OR it is on the edge of town **e.** Railway Parade. Because there are three railway stations on the street. **/ Language: a.** lake, sunset Ali, Paris **b.** principal, teachers, year Mr Green **c.** clouds, sky, rain **/ Spelling:** Parent **/ Word Building:** parent check **/ Sentences:** circle - **a, b, e, f, h, j, k, l / Partitioning: 1a.** 6 247 **b.** 3 186 **c.** 4 893 **d.** 2 750 **2a.** 6 x 10 000+ 2 x 1000+ 3 x 100+ 5 x 10+ 8 x 1 **b.** 8 x 10 000+6 x 1000+5x100+9x10+4x1 **/ Multiplying by 4: 1a.** 12, 12 **b.** 28, 28 **c.** 40, 40 **d.** 32, 32 **2.** 20, 12, 40, 0, 8, 24, 28, 36, 16, 32
Unit 5	**Understanding:** shade - **a.** 4; **b.** 1; **c.** 3; **d.** 2; **/ Interpreting: a.** Yes **b.** Yes **c.** Yes **d.** No **e.** No **f.** No **/ Language: a.** leave **b.** undo **c.** arrange **d.** sprinkle **e.** roll **/ Spelling:** Parent **/ Word Building: a.** off **b.** from **c.** from **d.** from **e.** off **f.** off **g.** from **h.** from **/ Sentences: a.** when the rains come we will be happy. b. In the winter, everybody feels cold **c.** With great haste, they ran for cover. **d.** because it looks green, which one is ripe? **e.** Last evening, the concert started early. **/ Data and Graphs: 1.** 14 **2.** 6th and 14th **3.** 41mm **4.** 6 days **5.** 14 **6.** 11th **7.** 27th **8.** 82mm **9.** No **10 a.** 12mm **b.** 17mm
Unit 6	**Understanding:** Poem: parent check Shade **a.** 2 **b.** 4 **c.** 3 **d.** 1 **/ Interpreting: a.** No **b.** Yes **c.** Yes **d.** Yes **e.** Yes **f.** No **/ Language: a.** backwards **b.** violently **c.** yesterday **d.** nearby **e.** because **/ Spelling:** Parent **/ Word Building: a.** crept **b.** waves **c.** disappear **d.** survive **e.** panic **f.** erupt **/ Syllables:** dis-a-ppear; tsu-na-mi; a-cros-tic **/ Sentences: a.** so **b.** and **c.** but **d.** so **e.** but **/ Mass: 1a.** 75kg **b.** 500g **c.** 75g **2a.** 80kg **b.** 60g **c.** 1 ½ kg **d.** 500g **e.** 2 000kg **f.** 250g **g.** 2 500kg **h.** 700g **i.** 250kg **j.** 25g **/ Square Centimetre: 1a.** = 14 **b.**= 13 **c.**= 16 **d.**=11 **2.** C
Unit 7	**Understanding:** tick **a. b. c. f. g. i. j / Interpreting: a.** It is on Bennelong Point **b.** ballet, pop concerts, **c.** The Danish Royal Family **d.** A funeral held for someone who has been an important member of the community **e.** It is in Sydney Harbour. **/ Language: a.** are **b.** not **c.** is **d.** will **e.** am **f.** have **g.** would **h.** is **i.** not **k.** will **/ Spelling:** Parent **/ Word Building:** Parent Sentences: **a.** their they **b.** you're yours **c.** theirs they're **d.** who's who's **e.** whose **/ Money: 1a.** \$8.30 **b.** \$23.85 **c.** \$9.55 **d.** \$105.20 **e.** \$68.40 **f.** \$55.85 **2a.** 10 **b.** 10 **c.** 20 **d.** 25 **/ Symmetry:** colour **a. c. e. f 2.** parent
Unit 8	**Understanding:** shade **a.** 4 **b.** 1 **c.** 2 **d.** 4 **/ Interpreting:** tick **a. b. c. d. e. / Language:** should, I think, OR I agree, If, on the other hand, would **/ Spelling:** parent **/ Word Building: a.** ac-com-mo-da-tion; **b.** con-sid-er-a-tion; **c.** re-cog-ni-tion; **d.** i-den-ti-fi-ca-tion; **e.** for-ma-tion; **f.** dis-a-gree-ment; **g.** a-ware-ness; **h.** state-ment; **i.** re-cog-nis-ing; **j.** cha-rac-ter-i-sa-tion; **/ Sentences: a.** I, you, he, me **b.** You, I , her **c.** Their, she, her **d.** yours, hers, his **e.** mine, yours, ours **/ Length: 1a.** 6cm **b.** 5cm **c.** 7cm **2.** Parent **/ Temperature: 1.** Pink **2.** 2
Unit 9	**Understanding: a.** no **b.** parent **c.** yes **d.** parent **e.** yes **/ Interpreting: a.** Sausages and Mash **b.** \$10 **c.** \$5 **d.** Sometimes kids don't like the same things as adults. **e.** mashed potatoes **/ Language: b.** who ran down the road **c.** where Paris lived. **d.** that I like best **e.** whose jacket was stolen **f.** to whom I am reading **g.** which was broken **h.** who went missing **/ Spelling:** Parent **/ Word Building:** parent check **/ Sentences: a.** The boy, who was sick, had books, pens, pencils and toys to use. **b.** The shoes, which were the wrong size, were returned for a refund. **c.** Red, purple, green and blue are colours that I like best. **/ Multiplying by 6: 1.** parent check **2.** 60, 12, 30, 18, 42, 24, 48, 36, 54, 0 **/ Multiplying by 7, 8 and 9: 1a.** 42 **b.** 32 **c.** 40 **d.** 27 **e.** 49 **f.** 64 **g.** 54 **h.** 56 **2.** 32, 64, 48, 80, 16, 72, 96, 40, 24, 56
Unit 10	**Understanding: a.** Victoria **b.** Chinese **c.** the government **d.** they burnt their licence to mine **e.** Eureka **/ Interpreting:** shade **a.** 2 **b.** 4 **c.** 3 **d.** 2 **/ Language: a.** At the beginning **b.** Now and then **c.** around the camps **d.** before long **e.** for their rights **f.** in Bendigo **/ Spelling:** Parent **/ Word Building: a.** a document **b.** given permission **c.** paper etc. **d.** a parked car **e.** one who depends on another for support **f.** to depend on something else **g.** of high moral truths **h.** one in charge, chief or head **i.** what one does **j.** to do or to act **/ Sentences: a.** Hobart **b.** Sydney **c.** Darwin **d.** Adelaide **e.** Brisbane **/ Capacity: 1a.** 11 L **b.** 250 mL **c.** 2L **2.** 55ml **3a.** 1L 250mL **b.** 22L 550mL **/ Location: 1 a. b.** parent check **2a.** East **b.** South **c.** West **d.** North

Answers

Unit 11	**Understanding:** tick - **a. b. c. d. i / Interpreting: a.** flat-footed **b.** reptile **c.** mammal **d.** webbed-feet **e.** back-bone **f.** hatches **/ Language: a.** warm-blooded The platypus, animal or monotreme **b.** only one of two, egg-laying mammals in the World **c.** female, platypus, young on her milk **d.** other, the, both; monotreme, echidna, Australia; **e.** all some mammals, back-bone, fur, bodies. **/ Spelling:** Parent **/ Word Building: a.** warm-blooded animal that suckles its young **b.** Carries its young in a pouch **c.** Lays eggs and suckles its young. **/ Sentences: a.** quickly down the street **b.** in the afternoon **c.** on the bus, this afternoon **d.** before the concert **e.** slowly but surely **f.** now and then **/ Decimal Fractions: 1a.** 0.5 **b.** 0.25 **c.** 0.1 **d.** 0.2 **e.** 0.4 **f.** 0.8 **g.** 0.75 **h.** 0.3 **i.** 0.6 **2a.** ½ **b.** 2/10 or l/5 **c.** 7/10 **d.** l/4 **e.** 1/10 **f.** 4/10 or 2/5 **g.** 2 9/10 **h.** 1¾ 3. 0.2, ¼, 0.3, ½ 0.7 **/ Factors and Multiples: 1a.** 24 **b.** 21 **c.** 90 **d.** 48 **e.** 56 **f.** 45 **g.** 27 **h.** 36 **2a.** 4 x 0, 4 x 1, 2 x 2; **b.** 7 x 0, 7 x 1; **c.** 5 x 0, 5 x 1; **d.** 3 x 0, 3 x 1; **3a.** True **b.** True **c.** True
Unit 12	**Understanding: a.** yes **b.** no **c.** yes **d.** yes **e.** yes **/ Interpreting: a.** There could be people and elderly people on the footpath who can't move out of the way quickly. They could fall over and get hurt. **b.** Knees get hurt, arms, legs and wrists can get broken as well as severe head injuries occur with long-lasting results. **/ Language: a.** will **b.** should **c.** certainly **d.** must **e.** because **f.** I know **/ Spelling:** Parent **/ Word Building:** parent check **/ Sentences: a.** until **b.** on **c.** before **d.** after **e.** in **f.** to **/ Prime and Multiples: 1.** circle - 1, 3, 5, 7, 11, 13, 17, 19 **2.** colour - 12, 16, 20, 28, 32, **/ Division: 1a.** 9 **b.** 4 **c.** 13 **d.** 6 **e.** 7 **f.** 8 **g.** 50 **h.** 33 **2a.** 7 **b.** 10 **c.** 4 **d.** 8 **e.** 3 **f.** 9 **g.** 6 **h.** 14
Unit 13	**Understanding: a.** 1986 **b.** 1971 **c.** 2000 **d.** 1986 **e.** 1970 **f.** 1971 **g.** 1986 **h.** 1973 **i.** 2000 **j.** 2020 **/ Interpreting: a.** permanent **b.** lunar **c.** historical **d.** explosion **e.** shuttle **f.** exploration **/ Language: a.** ISS **b.** NSW **c.** UN **d.** ISBN **/ Spelling:** Parent **/ Word Building:** parent check **/ Sentences: a.** did not **b.** shall not **c.** you are **d.** they will **e.** they are **f.** he is **/ Place Value: 1a.** 24 104 **b.** 62 035 **c.** 10 413 **d.** 50 312 **2a.** tens **b.** thousands **c.** ones **d.** hundreds **/ Decimal Fractions: 1a.** 0.32 **b.** 0.66 **2a.** 3231.14 **b.** 6042.56 **c.** 1342.15
Unit 14	**Understanding:** shade - **a.** 3 **b.** 4 **c.** 3 **d.** 2 **e.** 1 **f.** 2 **/ Interpreting: a.** Where the land meets the sea, **b.** billions of years **c.** all around between the Earth and the stratosphere **d.** sand and rocks or pebbles **/ Language: a.** silica, quartz, minerals, sand **b.** sunlight, atmosphere, particles, air **/ Spelling:** Parent **/ Word Building: a.** at-mos-phere; **b.** con-tain-ing; **c.** par-ti-cles; **d.** sub-stan-ces; **e.** phen-om-en-a; **f.** ex-plan-a-tion; **/ Unjumble: a.** atmosphere **b.** phenomena; **c.** pho-to-graph **/ Sentences: a.** He's going to buy the Game of Thrones. **b.** It's too late now so we'll miss our turn on the game. **c.** Why didn't your parents have Tom's dinner ready? **d.** He should've gone to school for today. **/ Multiplication: 1a.** 24 **b.** 16 **c.** 32 **d.** 60 **e.** 8 **f.** 48 **g.** 80 **h.** 12 **/ Division: 1a.** 9, 9, 27 **b.** 8, 8, 32 **c.** 9, 9, 54 **d.** 9, 9, 63 **/ Addition: 1a.** 6682 **b.** 8690 **/ Subtraction: 1a.** 3147 **b.** 5414
Unit 15	**Understanding: a.** F **b.** T **c.** F **d.** F **e.** F **f.** F **g.** F **h.** F **i.** T **j.** T **/ Interpreting: a.** He wants James to write and tell him about himself. It could be easier to use Email because it is quicker to get a reply. **b.** A boy. Because Henry is a boy and a boy would have more in common to talk about. **c.** He would like James to write to him and tell him all about himself. **/ Language: a.** children's **b.** mum's **c.** James' **d.** friends' **/ Spelling:** Parent **/ Word Building:** match - **a-l; b-k; c-h; d-l; e-m; f-g / Editing: a.** Many people found the trip too difficult. **b.** When the bright light was on it was good. **c.** Would you please sit in the right seat. **/ Sentences: a.** herd **b.** wood **c.** teaches **d.** teachers **/ Cross Section: 1.** parent **2.** slide **/ Lines: 1a.** oblique **b.** parallel **c.** horizontal **d.** perpendicular **e.** vertical 2 parent
Unit 16	**Understanding: a.** no **b.** yes **c.** no **d.** yes **e.** yes **f.** no **g.** yes **h.** no **/ Interpreting: a.** How to separate truth from fiction. **b.** write such a story with a group of friends **c.** Short Story Competition **d.** A newspaper **/ Language: a.** short, past Year 4 **b.** it, short **c.** biggest, many **d.** bright, good, this **e.** those, another **/ Spelling:** Parent **/ Word Building:** parent to check **/ Sentences: a.** statement **b.** question **c.** statement **d.** statement **e.** command **/ Chance: a.** likely **b.** unlikely **c.** 50/50 **d.** impossible **2a.** unlikely **b.** 50/50 **/ Angles: 1a.** reflex **b.** straight **c.** obtuse **d.** right **e.** obtuse **f.** right
Unit 17	**Understanding:** tick **a.** 2 **b.** 4 **c.** 1 **d.** 4, 1, 2,3 **/ Interpreting: a.** T **b.** T **c.** T **d.** T **e.** T **/ Language: a.** than **b.** however **c.** like **d.** as though **e.** therefore **/ Spelling:** Parent **/ Word Building: a.** argument **b.** description **c.** persuasion **d.** explanation **e.** information **f.** narration **g.** procedure **h.** exposition **i.** discussion **/ Sentences: a.** narrative **b.** argument **c.** description **d.** factual recount **e.** procedure **/ Capacity: 1a.** 50mL **b.** 300mL **c.** 450mL **d.** 250mL **2.** shade **a.** 25L **b.** 250mL **/ Time: 1a.** 2:37 **b.** 8:26 **c.** 2:56 **2a.** 10:45 **b.** 1:35 **3.** 9:32
Unit 18	**Understanding: a.** 8:30pm **b.** Yes **c.** Yes **d.** No **e.** No **/ Interpreting:** tick - **a, b, d, e / Language:** match - **a-g; b-l; c-j; d-h; e-f / Spelling:** Parent **/ Word Building:** parent check **/ Sentences: a.** definitely **b.** always **c.** surely **d.** could, definitely **e.** certain, no doubt **/ Fractions: 1.** colour - **a.** 4 parts **b.** 5parts **c.** 2 parts **2a.** 4/5 **b.** ½ **c.** ½ **d.** ½ **e.** 2/5 **f.** ¾ **g.** 2 **h.** 2 **/ X and ÷ : 1a.** 16, 28, 48, 36, 20, 32 **b.** 2, 18, 12, 6, 24, 36 **2a.** 12 **b.** 9 **c.** 7 **d.** 6
Unit 19	**Understanding: a.** opinion **b.** fact **c.** fact **d.** opinion **e.** fact **/ Interpreting: a.**T **b.** F **c.** T **d.** F **e.** F **f.** F **g.** T **h.** T **i.** T **j.** T **/ Language: a.** is **b.** was **c.** were **d.** are **e.** am **/ Spelling:** Parent **/ Word Building:** parent to check **/ Word meaning: a.** A story attempting to explain a natural phenomena. **b.** A confusing, inter-connecting group of circular paths hard to find a way out of. **/ Sentences: a.** labyrinth **b.** prisoners **c.** myth **d.** invented **e.** feathers **/ Decimal Fractions:** 1a. 25/100 **b.** 62/100 **c.** 77/100 **2a.** 0.75 **b.** 0.7 **c.** 0.5 **d.** 0.8 **e.** 0.85 **f.** 0.72 **3.** 0.5 **/ Place Value: 1a.** 61 692 **b.** 3 802 **c.** 7 197 **d.** 62 788 **2a.** hundreds **b.** 8 tens **c.** 3 tens of thousands **3a.** 23 567 **b.**15 789 **c.** 23 678 **d.** 2 567

Answers

Unit 20	**Understanding: a.** No **b.** Yes **c.** No **d.** Yes **e.** Yes **/ Interpreting: a.** It's in the country. It has a tractor and a ride-on mower, to cut lots of grass. **b.** To be used in grandma's garden. **c.** 2 **d.** There are cans of soft drink. **e.** They have been collected over many years because they might come in handy one day. **/ Language: a.** biggest **b.** longest **c.** lightest **d.** best, better **e.** bad, worse, worst. **/ Spelling:** Parent **/ Word Building:** parent to check **Syllables: h.** con-di-tion **i.** col-lec-tion **/ Sentences: a.** amazing **b.** lathe **c.** tractor **d.** wood splitter **e.** collection **/ Mixed Additions: 1a.** $302.03 **b.** $789.55 **c.** $399.93 **2.** 134, 223, 106, 99, 173, 118, 81, 153, 318, 145, 111 **/ Mixed Bag: 1a.** 1 **b.** 4:50pm **c.** $13.75 **d.** 0.8 **2.** 27 **3a.** 450 **b.** 2 860 **c.** 100 **d.** 0.92
Unit 21	**Understanding: a.** T **b.** T **c.** T **d.** F **e.** T **/ Interpreting:** shade - **a.** 3 **b.** 1 **c.** 2 **d.** 1 **/ Language: a.** am doing **b.** are singing **c.** are running **d.** is ringing **/ Spelling:** Parent **/ Word Building: a.** their **b.** they're **c.** their **d.** there **e.** there **f.** They're/ Parent check 'qu' words **/ Sentences: a.** wished **b.** thought, believe **c.** remember **d.** wonder, feel **e.** consider, upset **/ Locations: 1.** parent to check **2a.** G5 **b.** H4 **c.** B8 **d.** B3 **e.** E6 **f.** I8 **g.** E3 **h.** C5 **i.** D1
Unit 22	**Understanding:** order - **d, b, f, a, e, c / Interpreting: a.** Yes **b.** parent **c.** Yes **d.** Yes **e.** Yes **/ Language: a.** cards **b.** bananas **c.** sheep **d.** bees **e.** cattle **f.** children **g.** ants **h.** kittens **i.** grapes **j.** players **/ Spelling:** Parent **/ Word Building:** match - **a - k, b - l, c - m, d - l, e - h, f - n, g - j / Homophones:** flowers, flour **/ Sentences: a.** didn't **b.** weren't **c.** couldn't **d.** shan't, they'll **e.** won't **/ Capacity: 1a.** 25mL **b.** 350ml **c.** 18mL **d.** 490mL **2a.** 8000mL **b.** 2500mL **c.** 500mL **d.** 750mL **/ Money: 1a.** $20.40 **b.** $62.60 **c.** $10 **d.** $2.30 **2.** $1.25
Unit 23	**Understanding: a.** F **b.** O **c.** O **d.** F **e.** F **f.** F **g.** F **/ Interpreting:** tick - **a, b, c, d, e, / Language: a.** one, ~~are~~ **b.** gang, ~~were~~, **c.** litter, ~~are~~, **d.** choir, ~~are~~, **e.** neighbour, ~~are~~; herd, ~~are~~, **/ Spelling:** Parent **/ Word Building:** match - **a - j; b - l; c - d - g; e - h / Prefixes: a.** become **b.** beware **c.** because **/ Sentences: a.** were running, **b.** was getting **c.** were looking **d.** was swimming **e.** were reading **/ Shapes and Angles: 1a.** square **b.** triangle **c.** rectangle **d.** triangle **e.** triangle **2a.** 9 **b.** 1 **c.** 9 **/ Perimeter: 1a.** 8 cm **b.** 9 cm **c.** 10 cm **d.** 10 cm **2.** 16 cm
Unit 24	**Understanding: a.** F **b.** F **c.** T **d.** F **e.** T **f.** F **g.** T **h.** T **/ Interpreting: a.** It doesn't say. **b.** By sending an Email **c.** samt08@gmail.com **d.** gmail.com **e.** as soon as possible **/ Language: b.** has rung **c.** have seen **d.** have done **e.** has seen **/ Spelling:** Parent **/ Word Building: a.** loop, tie **b.** to have knowledge of **c.** implement to cut with **d.** to form with hands **e.** a noble man **f.** a dishonest fellow **g.** to hold in high esteem, high praise **h.** truthful **i.** to hold office without pay **j.** conferring honour **/ Sentences: a.** buy **b.** bring **c.** bought **d.** brought **e.** Bring, bought **/ Fractions: 1.a.** 3/8 **b.** 8/10 OR 4/5 **c.** 2/5 **d.** ¾ **2.** 17/100 **3.** 0.64 **/ Division: 1a.** 8 **b.** 8 **c.** 8 **d.** 9 **e.** 36 **f.** 42 **g.** 9 **h.** 9 **2a.** 6 **b.** 8 **c.** 9 **d.** 24 **e.** 13 **f.** 21
Unit 25	**Understanding:** shade - **a.** 2 **b.** 3 **c.** 4 **d.** 2 **/ Interpreting: a.** So they do not have to spend a lot of money at Christmas. OR So they are sure to have the toys they want at Christmas. **b.** a list of items with prices **c.** Toy sales like this are very popular, **d.** So people will buy them and stocks will go. **e.** Either on-line or in- store. **/ Language: a.** will have **b.** will go **c.** will finish **d.** will play **/ Spelling:** Parent **/ Word Building:** parent check **a-e; Past tense verbs: a.** brought **b.** bought **c.** ran **d.** saw **/ Sentences: a.** bought **b.** ran **c.** saw **d.** brought **/ Decimals: 1.** l/10, 0.3, 4/10, ½, 7/10, 4/5 **2a.** 3.9 **b.** 7.7 **c.** 28.9 **d.** 9.5 **3a.** $58.85 **b.** $ 74.79 **c.** $ 59.97 **/ X and ÷ Equivalents**:**1a.** 6, 6 **b.** 7, 7 **2a.** 100 **b.** 111 **c.** 372 **d.** 24 **e.** 13 **f.** 21 **3.** 7.
Unit 26	**Understanding: a.** Yes **b.** Yes **c.** No **d.** No **e.** Yes **f.** Yes **g.** No **h.** No **/ Interpreting: a.** To write a person's name. **b.** My parents, grandparents or some other relative. **c.** Because it is the polite thing to do and it was a request on the invitation. **d.** Yes, so arrangements can be made for seating and catering. **e.** No, because you would be one of the performers. **/ Language: a.** upset **b.** enjoy **c.** calm **d.** hurt **e.** worry **/ Spelling:** Parent **/ Word Building:** parent to check **/ tSyllables: a.** in-vi-ta-tion; **b.** ar-range-ments; **c.** com-mit-tee **/ Sentences: a.** pleasure **b.** amusement **c.** sadness **/ Maps and Location: 1a.** H9 **b.** church **c.** D4 **d.** H1 **e.** A6 **f.** G-H 5-6 **g.** railway station **h.** one **i.** N-S
Unit 27	**Understanding: a.** T **b.** T **c.** T **d.** T **e.** T **/ Interpreting: a.** Name the animals on the Australian Coat of Arms. **b.** What is the purpose of the Sydney Harbour Bridge? **c.** How many points on the large star on the Australian Flag and what does each one represent? **d.** Where is Uluru and what is it? **/ Language: a.** above **b.** beyond **c.** between **d.** close **e.** nearby **/ Spelling:** Parent **/ Word Building: a.** two **b.** to, too **c.** to **d.** two, to **e.** two, too **f.** too, to **g.** two **h.** to, to **i.** to, two, too **j.** two, to / Sentences: **a.** Parliament **b.** National **c.** Flag **d.** aboriginal, Uluru **/ Shopping: 1a.** $2.97 + $1.09 + $3.33 + $ 2.97 = $10.35 **2a.** $15 .60 **b.** $13.70 **/ Money and Change: 1a.** $ 10.30 **b.** $2.65 **c.** $35.45 **d.** 28.40 **2.** $5.45
Unit 28	**Understanding:** tick - **a, b, c, d, e, f. Interpreting:** tick - **a, b, c, e, f, g, h / Language: a.** transparent **b.** moults **c.** muscles, abdomen **d.** habitats **/ Spelling:** Parent **/ Word Building: a.** to come out of **b.** to shed or loose **c.** the natural environment of an animal **d.** the belly **e.** can be seen through **f.** fibres connecting body parts. **/ Syllables:** disappears - habitat - transparent - abdomen - **/ Sentences: a.** tiny, black **b.** many **c.** tiny, dark **d.** five to six **e.** soft, pale, long **f.** transparent, see-through g. loud h. hot, cool **/ Time and Travel: 1a.** 1 hour 17 minutes **b.** 5 hours 55 minutes **c.** 7:45 am **d.** 3 hours 10 minutes **e.** 50 minutes **f.** 8:02 am **2a.** 3:05 pm **b.** 2 hours 35 minutes
Unit 29	**Understanding:** shade - **a.** 3 **b.** 2 **c.** 4 **d.** 3 **/ Spelling:** Parent **/ Word Building:** parent check
Unit 30	**Adjective or Adverb: 1a.** adjective, adverb **b.** adjective, adverb **c.** adjective, adverb **Demonstrative Adjectives: 2a.** these **b.** this **c.** that **d.** these **Gender: 3a.** He is late for his appointment and his mother is late too. **b.** My aunty is very ill and she will be in hospital until she is well. **c.** There were twenty girls and five boys in the class and a female teacher. **Punctuation: 4a.** The National Capital of Australia is Canberra. **b.** We are going to The Capitol to see The Sound of Music. **c.** Lisa and Irene were having lunch at The Broadbeach Hotel. **/ Area: 1a.** cm2 **b.** m2 **c,** cm2 **d.** cm2 **e.** m2 Factors: **1a.** 1x12; 2x6; 3x4; **b.** 1x20; 2x10; 4x5; **c.** 1x18; 2x9; 3x6; **2a.** 7, 4, 8, 10, 5, 9 **b.** 5, 7, 4, 9, 6, 3, 10, 8